Techniques for Evaluating and Improving Instruction

Lawrence M. Aleamoni, *Editor*
University of Arizona

NEW DIRECTIONS FOR TEACHING AND LEARNING
KENNETH E. EBLE, *Editor-in-Chief*
University of Utah, Salt Lake City

Number 31, Fall 1987

Paperback sourcebooks in
The Jossey-Bass Higher Education Series

Jossey-Bass Inc., Publishers
San Francisco • London

Lawrence M. Aleamoni (ed.).
Techniques for Evaluating and Improving Instruction.
New Directions for Teaching and Learning, no. 31.
San Francisco: Jossey-Bass, 1987.

New Directions for Teaching and Learning
Kenneth E. Eble, *Editor-in-Chief*

New Directions for Teaching and Learning is published quarterly
by Jossey-Bass Inc., Publishers. POSTMASTER: Send address
changes to Jossey-Bass Inc., Publishers, 433 California Street,
San Francisco, California 94104.

Editorial correspondence should be sent to the Editor-in-Chief,
Kenneth E. Eble, Department of English, University of Utah,
Salt Lake City, Utah 84112.

Library of Congress Catalog Card Number LC 85-644763

International Standard Serial Number ISSN 0271-0633

International Standard Book Number ISBN 1-55542-935-1

Cover art by WILLI BAUM

Ordering Information

The paperback sourcebooks listed below are published quarterly and can be ordered either by subscription or single copy.

Subscriptions cost $48.00 per year for institutions, agencies, and libraries. Individuals can subscribe at the special rate of $36.00 per year *if payment is by personal check.* (Note that the full rate of $48.00 applies if payment is by institutional check, even if the subscription is designated for an individual.) Standing orders are accepted.

Single copies are available at $11.95 when payment accompanies order. (California, New Jersey, New York, and Washington, D.C., residents please include appropriate sales tax.) For billed orders, cost per copy is $11.95 plus postage and handling.

Substantial discounts are offered to organizations and individuals wishing to purchase bulk quantities of Jossey-Bass sourcebooks. Please inquire.

Please note that these prices are for the academic year 1987–1988 and are subject to change without notice. Also, some titles may be out of print and therefore not available for sale.

To ensure correct and prompt delivery, all orders must give either the *name of an individual* or an *official purchase order number.* Please submit your order as follows:

Subscriptions: specify series and year subscription is to begin.
Single Copies: specify sourcebook code (such as, TL1) and first two words of title.

Mail orders for United States and Possessions, Latin America, Canada, Japan, Australia, and New Zealand to:
   Jossey-Bass Inc., Publishers
   433 California Street
   San Francisco, California 94104

Mail orders for all other parts of the world to:
   Jossey-Bass Limited
   28 Banner Street
   London EC1Y 8QE

New Directions for Teaching and Learning Series
Kenneth E. Eble, *Editor-in-Chief*

TL1   *Improving Teaching Styles,* Kenneth E. Eble
TL2   *Learning, Cognition, and College Teaching,* Wilbert J. McKeachie
TL3   *Fostering Critical Thinking,* Robert E. Young

TL4   *Learning About Teaching,* John F. Noonan
TL5   *The Administrator's Role in Effective Teaching,* Alan E. Guskin
TL6   *Liberal Learning and Careers,* Charles S. Green III, Richard G. Salem
TL7   *New Perspectives on Teaching and Learning,* Warren Bryan Martin
TL8   *Interdisciplinary Teaching,* Alvin M. White
TL9   *Expanding Learning Through New Communications Technologies,* Christopher K. Knapper
TL10 *Motivating Professors to Teach Effectively,* James L. Bess
TL11 *Practices That Improve Teaching Evaluation,* Grace French-Lazovik
TL12 *Teaching Writing in All Disciplines,* C. Williams Griffin
TL13 *Teaching Values and Ethics in College,* Michael J. Collins
TL14 *Learning in Groups,* Clark Bouton, Russell Y. Garth
TL15 *Revitalizing Teaching Through Faculty Development,* Paul A. Lacey
TL16 *Teaching Minority Students,* James H. Cones III, John F. Noonan, Denise Janha
TL17 *The First Year of College Teaching,* L. Dee Fink
TL18 *Increasing the Teaching Role of Academic Libraries,* Thomas G. Kirk
TL19 *Teaching and Aging,* Chandra M. N. Mehrotra
TL20 *Rejuvenating Introductory Courses,* Karen I. Spear
TL21 *Teaching as Though Students Mattered,* Joseph Katz
TL22 *Strengthening the Teaching Assistant Faculty,* John D. W. Andrews
TL23 *Using Research to Improve Teaching,* Janet C. Donald, Arthur M. Sullivan
TL24 *College-School Collaboration: Appraising the Major Approaches,* William T. Daly
TL25 *Fostering Academic Excellence Through Honors Programs,* Paul G. Friedman, Reva Jenkins-Friedman
TL26 *Communicating in College Classrooms,* Jean M. Civikly
TL27 *Improving Teacher Education,* Eva C. Galambos
TL28 *Distinguished Teachers on Effective Teaching,* Peter G. Beidler
TL29 *Coping with Faculty Stress,* Peter Seldin
TL30 *Developing Critical Thinking and Problem-Solving Abilities,* James E. Stice

Contents

Editor's Notes   1
Lawrence M. Aleamoni

1. Can Evaluating Instruction Improve Teaching?   3
W. J. McKeachie
Evaluation alone will probably not improve teaching, but, when it is
accompanied by feedback, information about teaching and learning, and
work with a knowledgeable consultant, evaluation may lead to improvement.

2. Toward Excellence in Teaching   9
Robert C. Wilson
Underlying all attempts to improve teaching is the process of getting faculty to accept specific suggestions and put them into practice. A pool of
good ideas about teaching is not difficult to generate, and experienced
consultants can help faculty adopt some of these ideas.

3. Typical Faculty Concerns About Student Evaluation of   25
Teaching
Lawrence M. Aleamoni
Eight faculty concerns are presented, along with research evidence that
addresses them.

4. Using Student Ratings to Improve Instruction   33
Joseph J. Stevens
Instructional improvement programs are most likely to be effective if, in
addition to providing feedback to instructors, there is a system of institutional support, reward, and training.

5. The Role of Student Government in Faculty Evaluation   39
Raoul A. Arreola
Student governments played an important role in the development of faculty evaluation programs. Suggestions are made about the value of student
governments in today's comprehensive faculty evaluation programs.

6. Formative and Summative Evaluation: Parody or Paradox?   47
John A. Centra
Six different topics (student ratings, colleague evaluations, definitions of
good teaching, teacher examinations, evaluations of research and scholarship, and the politics of evaluation) are covered in trying to answer this
question.

7. Instructional Evaluation as a Feedback Process   57
Doron H. Gil

Consultants possessing process as well as interpersonal skills should be used to provide feedback to instructors about the meaning of their instructional evaluations.

8. A Faculty Evaluation Model for Community and Junior   65
Colleges
Raoul A. Arreola

A procedure for developing a comprehensive faculty evaluation program is described with examples of various components. Procedures for implementing such a program are discussed.

9. Some Practical Approaches for Faculty and Administrators   75
Lawrence M. Aleamoni

Suggestions on how to develop comprehensive systems of instructional improvement and evaluation are offered.

10. Concluding Comments   79
Lawrence M. Aleamoni

The unifying threads running through the preceding chapters are highlighted.

11. Additional Sources and Information   83
Joseph J. Stevens

Annotated references provide further information on instructional evaluation and improvement.

Index   93

Editor's Notes

This sourcebook represents a collection of presentations made at the First National Conference on Instructional Improvement and Evaluation Techniques for Colleges and Universities, February 15–17, 1984, in Tucson, Arizona. The conference was sponsored by the University of Arizona's Office of Instructional Research and Development and the Department of Educational Psychology. Recent interest in evaluating instruction for the purposes of improvement and administrative decision making has rekindled concerns at the state and national levels. The presentations by nationally known resource persons reflect the latest issues and developments in the field. The aim of this volume is to provide faculty and administrators with practical approaches for instructional improvement and evaluation programs.

In the first chapter, Wilbert McKeachie stresses the need for instructional development consultants to be versed in the research on and theories of teaching and learning if these consultants are to be effective in their instructional improvement efforts. In the second chapter, Robert Wilson describes an approach used at the University of California, Berkeley, to generate a pool of good ideas for helping faculty improve their teaching based on information from past recipients of the campus Distinguished Teaching Award. He then describes how experienced consultants used these ideas with faculty.

Chapters three through five discuss student evaluations. In Chapter Three, I address eight concerns that are brought up often by faculty and administrators in resisting or opposing student ratings of teachers. Each of these concerns is confronted with research evidence available from the past sixty-three years. Joseph Stevens, in Chapter Four, accepts the widespread use of student ratings but focuses on how they might best be used for instructional improvement. While the research literature neither proves nor disproves the effectiveness of student ratings in improving teacher performance, it does point to the relative ineffectiveness of student ratings if they are unaccompanied by a more comprehensive support system. Raoul Arreola, in Chapter Five, examines the role that student government has played in fostering student ratings. He then suggests how student governments can continue to play a role in the development of comprehensive faculty evaluation programs aimed at improvements in teaching and learning.

The discussion of student ratings and their effectiveness in improving teaching leads naturally to the larger question of the relationship between evaluation measures used to support decisions about retention,

1

promotion, and tenure and those used to provide feedback to the faculty for the purpose of improvement. John Centra, in Chapter Six, surveys the broad territory of both evaluating faculty and assisting them in developing their skills. Doron Gil argues, in the following chapter, that feedback should be the primary purpose of the various measures employed to evaluate teaching.

The interest in and need for evaluating teaching exists at every level of education; in Chapter Eight, Raoul Arreola offers a faculty evaluation model that has found particular acceptance in junior and community colleges. Crucial problems of evaluating faculty services in any institution are not only those of identifying and measuring teaching effectiveness but also of reaching agreement as to the weight to be placed on various faculty responsibilities.

In the last substantive chapter, I look at the problems of developing comprehensive systems of instructional evaluation. Within a comprehensive system, it should be possible to furnish better evidence of teaching performance as well as to provide faculty with information and incentives for improved performance.

A brief look back at the major themes of the sourcebook's chapters and an extensive annotated bibliography of current research on instructional evaluation and improvement conclude the book.

Lawrence M. Aleamoni
Editor

Lawrence M. Aleamoni is professor of educational psychology and director of the Office of Instructional Research and Development at the University of Arizona.

An experienced consultant can foster trust, offer
encouragement, and provide guided practice in order
to help faculty improve their teaching techniques.

Can Evaluating Instruction Improve Teaching?

W. J. McKeachie

This chapter was developed in response to a frequently raised question: "Is instructional improvement a viable outcome of instructional evaluation?" The obvious answer is "yes," but equally obvious is the fact that many educators have doubts about that answer. Certainly the research evidence does not support the proposition that instituting instructional evaluation is the quick and easy road to the improvement of teaching. Peter Cohen's (1980) meta-analysis of student-rating research suggests that instituting student ratings typically but *not invariably* produces some improvement in teaching. Cohen cites Aleamoni's (1978) research as one of the studies indicating that improvement is much more likely when the ratings are discussed with a consultant.

Since faculty members are usually individuals with strong personal interests and needs that influence their teaching styles, they must be provided with clear intellectual rationale for changes in their procedures if improvements are to be made. It helps, then, if faculty members understand theories of teaching and learning, but this understanding alone is not sufficient. Faculty also need opportunities to develop skills and to practice these skills with a minimum risk of embarrassment in order to make improvements.

To help teachers improve, I suggest: first, that we look at the moti-

L. M. Aleamoni (ed.). *Techniques for Evaluating and Improving Instruction.*
New Directions for Teaching and Learning, no. 31. San Francisco: Jossey-Bass, Fall 1987.

vation of the individual and attempt to provide ways in which teaching can become more rewarding; second, that we provide a cognitive basis for change by giving the individual some understanding of theories of teaching and learning; and, third, that we provide some practice in developing new skills.

The Uses of Instructional Evaluation

Now, what kinds of processes do we use to achieve these three goals? And how does instructional evaluation fit in? In many cases, not much evaluation is needed; individuals who are in real difficulty in their teaching know—and their colleagues know—that things are not going well. However, instructional evaluation may be helpful, not so much in determining whether or not teaching is less than optimal, but in identifying specifically where the problems lie. This is the crucial point in differentiating instructional evaluation used for improvement from instructional evaluation used for personnel decisions. For personnel decisions, one needs some index of overall teaching effectiveness in order to determine whether the faculty member should be promoted or should receive a merit increase. For instructional improvement, evaluation serves as a diagnostic tool. The more precise its definition of particular areas of difficulty, the more likely it is that an appropriate prescription for change can be developed.

Appropriate Evaluation Techniques

A broader range of techniques is appropriate when evaluation is used to encourage instructional improvement but not when it is used to help make personnel decisions. For personnel purposes, faculty and administrators rightfully have great concerns about the validity and reliability of evaluation data. These concerns are not as crucial when we are dealing with instructional improvement because the information collected serves simply as a source of hypotheses about what procedures an instructor might try in order to improve. The consequences of information that is less than optimally valid or reliable are less permanent and less crucial to the individual instructor than are the consequences of unreliable or invalid information used in making a personnel decision.

What kinds of evaluation data are useful? As already mentioned, specific information is more helpful than general information, and, while there is a temptation to say that the more information available, the better, it is doubtful that this is actually true. If a large quantity of information is available, faculty who are trying to improve their teaching may be so overwhelmed that they will not be able to select those items that can be most helpful to them. For example, in some of the early trials of videotape recording of classes, it appeared that individuals seeing themselves on television were so distracted by their mannerisms and other superficial aspects of their television appearance that they had difficulty identifying the instructional features needing improvement. Viewing the videotape with a consultant who could point out salient characteristics proved to be more effective than viewing it alone.

Similarly, large numbers of items in student-rating forms are likely simply to "snow" the teacher. In some of our research (Kulik and Kulik, 1974), we believed it to be helpful to group items into general factors and then identify which factors required attention; the instructor could then focus on just those individual items that related to the selected areas of concern.

With student ratings, it is also important for the teachers themselves to identify characteristics specific to their classes about which they have some concern. While this process may result in their missing areas in which they have blind spots, it does have a motivational advantage: If teachers have asked for the information, they are more likely to respond to it than if the ratings are on a standard scale that they see as inapplicable to their particular classes.

The notion of asking the teacher to think about his or her goals for the course and to relate the items on the student questionnaire to these goals is appealing since it provides a context for interpreting the results; the rationale for change is obvious if the achievement of the goals seems to be less than desired.

Students' written comments often are helpful in identifying specifics that might not appear on the generalized rating scales. Students also may have useful suggestions about possible ways to improve the teacher's style.

Braskamp and others (1983) have used the technique of interviewing class members as a group. An instructional development specialist is invited to the class by the teacher and asks the class members about their impressions of the teacher. As a specialist in teaching, he or she is able to probe for specific aspects of diagnosis that the students might not include on ratings. The group interview technique allows the specialist to determine how widely shared particular dissatisfactions are and the degree to which students have common perceptions of the teacher. By asking students for examples to support the comments or criticisms they make, the specialist is able to obtain more concrete data than are usually found in student ratings—or, for that matter, in most other forms of instructional evaluation.

Peer observations are another source of evaluation data. Although such observations are not very useful for personnel purposes because of the lack of reliability and typically high ratings, they can be quite useful for encouraging improvement since they provide faculty with an opportunity to talk with colleagues and obtain feedback—an opportunity that is relatively rare in most academic contexts.

In discussing sources of data, we should not neglect the instructors' self-evaluations. Teachers can be motivated to improve when a discrepancy exists between their perceptions of themselves and the students' perceptions. Thus, a comparison between self-evaluative data and data gathered by other means may provide the starting point for the process leading to change.

The Value of a Consultant

The collection of data for instructional improvement should be distinguished from the evaluation of those data. Whereas, in personnel decisions, the data must ultimately be evaluated by a decision-making group such as a departmental promotions committee, in instructional improvement the impact of the data finally depends on the faculty member's own evaluation of them. As I have already suggested, this evaluation is less likely to be effective if it is carried out alone than if the individual has help from an experienced consultant.

A consultant can do three things: First, he or she can help identify particularly important information provided in the data, separating critical information from superficial information. Second, the consultant can provide hope and encouragement. All too often feedback fails because it discourages the individual and increases his or her sense of anxiety and hopelessness. And, third, a consultant can provide suggestions about what to do about the data—for example, suggestions about alternative methods of teaching that may be more productive than those used in the past.

Naturally, a consultant is likely to be more effective if he or she has experience in teaching, is supportive of and trusted by the individual, and is not in a position to use the information in a way that might be harmful to the individual. Research in business (McKeachie and others, 1980) suggests that subordinates are less likely to ask their supervisors for help when the supervisor recommends salary increases, since any indication of inadequacy might reflect unfavorably on them in decisions about promotions or pay. Thus, something like Wilson's use of retired faculty members as mentors, outlined in Chapter Two, might be particularly helpful for instructional improvement.

A Successful Model

At the University of Michigan, a faculty member in the Department of Communications and at the Center for Research on Learning and Teaching has been particularly effective in working with other faculty on problems of communication and speaking. When asked what sorts of things he does in his workshops to bring about such marked changes, he points to the sense of trust that he establishes. Because of this trust, the participants realize that, as they give practice lectures, they are not going to be embarrassed or put down by the leader or by other members of the group; rather, they know that they will be supported, encouraged, and given useful suggestions.

The second secret of his success lies in the practice lectures themselves. In the past, efforts to help faculty members and graduate students improve their teaching have lacked opportunities for skill development and practice. Frequently, consultants are able to help individuals identify a problem and to offer alternatives they might try, but the faculty have not had the chance to master the new techniques. If a faculty member knows what to do but feels incapable of doing it, no change is likely to occur.

Thus, trust, encouragement, and guided practice are three crucial factors that help determine whether actual improvement will result from the evaluation of teaching.

References

Aleamoni, L. M. "The Usefulness of Student Evaluations in Improving College Teaching." *Instructional Science,* 1978, 7, 95–105.
Braskamp, L. A., Brandenburg, D. C., Kohen, E., Ory, J. C., and Mayberry, P. W. *Guidebook for Evaluating Instructional Effectiveness.* Urbana: Measurement and Research Division, Office of Instructional Resources, University of Illinois, 1983.
Cohen, P. A. "Effectiveness of Student-Rating Feedback for Improving College Instruction: A Meta-Analysis of Findings." *Research in Higher Education,* 1980, 13 (4), 321–341.
Kulik, J. A., and Kulik, C.L.C. "Student Ratings of Instruction." *Teaching of Psychology,* 1974, 1, 51–57.
McKeachie, W. J., Lin, Y-G., Daugherty, M., Moffett, M., Neigler, C., Nork, J., Walz, M., and Baldwin, R. "Using Student Ratings and Consultation to Improve Instruction." *British Journal of Educational Psychology,* 1980, 50, 168–174.

W. J. McKeachie is a professor of psychology and was director of the Center for Research on Learning and Teaching from 1975 to 1983 at the University of Michigan.

Distinguished teaching faculty can help develop a pool of good ideas for improving teaching.

Toward Excellence in Teaching

Robert C. Wilson

This chapter describes a successful approach to helping faculty members improve their teaching that was developed at the University of California, Berkeley, from 1979 to 1982. This approach led to related projects that are still being studied. All of the projects described were completed under the auspices of the Council on Educational Development, a committee of the academic senate that is chaired by an administrator.

The first of these projects began in 1979 with the establishment of the Teaching Evaluation Consultation Service (TECS). TECS researched a consultation process designed to help faculty members improve instruction. The consultants were the assistant director of Teaching Innovation and Evaluation Services, an assistant research psychologist, and the research psychologist and director.

Getting Good Ideas from Excellent Teachers

TECS's first task was to develop a pool of good ideas for helping faculty improve their teaching. A look at the literature on teaching proved to be disappointing. We decided to ask past recipients of the campus's Distinguished Teaching Award for permission to administer our thirty-item Student Description of Teaching questionnaire in one of their classes.

L. M. Aleamoni (ed.). *Techniques for Evaluating and Improving Instruction.*
New Directions for Teaching and Learning, no. 31. San Francisco: Jossey-Bass, Fall 1987.

We then interviewed these instructors about the half-dozen items students said were most descriptive of their teaching. Figure 1 exhibits the questions contained in the Student Description of Teaching questionnaire.

In the interview, a consultant might say to a faculty member in physics, for example, "Your students give you a mean of 4.8 on a 5-point scale on the item 'knows if the class is understanding him/her or not.' Can you tell me anything you do that would lead students to say that this is one of the most descriptive features of your teaching?" "Sure," the faculty member might respond, "minute papers." "What's a minute paper?" The consultant asks. "Well, several times during the term—actually, about once a week—I come to class a little early. I write on the board:

1. What is the most significant thing you learned today?
2. What question is uppermost in your mind at the end of this class session?

"Then I turn around and make my presentation for forty-nine minutes. One minute before the end of the period, I say to the class, 'Pull out a piece of paper. I will give you one minute to answer these two questions.'

I started doing this as a sort of academically respectable way of taking roll. The students signed the papers and passed them to the center aisle. I picked them up on my way out of class. I handed them to my reader, and he checked off the names of those people who turned them in.

"Then one day I started reading some of the papers, and I found I could tell whether I was getting my point across. I could also tell what kinds of difficulties students were having. Clarifying difficult points at the next class meeting was easy.

"Early identification of students who were in real difficulty was also possible. If a student gave me off-the-wall responses, I invited him or her to come see me. One of the common problems was when a student had the course prerequisites on paper but not in his or her head. Besides, the minute-paper process causes students to listen more actively. All during the class session they are saying to themselves, 'Is this the most significant thing I am going to learn today?' And, toward the end of the hour, they have to wonder, 'Well, what question *is* uppermost in my mind at the end of this session?'

"Physics students do not get much opportunity to write, and their writing improves. The responses I get in the last week of the term are more articulate, more sophisticated, and longer than the ones I get at the beginning of the term."

Suggestions such as this, which came out of the interviews, were written up in an established format. Figures 2 and 3 show this format for two other teaching ideas. Altogether, about 450 ideas were collected and keyed to the thirty items on the questionnaire.

Figure 1. Student Description of Teaching

	Not at all descriptive				Very descriptive	N/A
1. Discusses points of view other than his/her own	1	2	3	4	5	( )
2. Contrasts implications of various theories	1	2	3	4	5	( )
3. Discusses recent developments in the field	1	2	3	4	5	( )
4. Gives references for more interesting and involved points	1	2	3	4	5	( )
5. Emphasizes conceptual understanding	1	2	3	4	5	( )
6. Explains clearly	1	2	3	4	5	( )
7. Is well prepared	1	2	3	4	5	( )
8. Gives lectures that are easy to outline	1	2	3	4	5	( )
9. Summarizes major points	1	2	3	4	5	( )
10. States objectives for each class session	1	2	3	4	5	( )
11. Identifies what he/she considers important	1	2	3	4	5	( )
12. Encourages class discussion	1	2	3	4	5	( )
13. Invites students to share their knowledge and experiences	1	2	3	4	5	( )
14. Invites criticism of his/her own ideas	1	2	3	4	5	( )
15. Knows if the class is understanding him/her or not	1	2	3	4	5	( )
16. Has students apply concepts to demonstrate understanding	1	2	3	4	5	( )
17. Knows when students are bored	1	2	3	4	5	( )
18. Has genuine interest in students	1	2	3	4	5	( )
19. Gives personal help to students having difficulties in course	1	2	3	4	5	( )
20. Relates to students as individuals	1	2	3	4	5	( )
21. Is accessible to students out of class	1	2	3	4	5	( )
22. Has an interesting style of presentation	1	2	3	4	5	( )
23. Is enthusiastic about his/her subject	1	2	3	4	5	( )
24. Varies the speed and tone of his/her voice	1	2	3	4	5	( )
25. Has interest in and concern for the quality of his/her teaching	1	2	3	4	5	( )
26. Motivates students to do their best work	1	2	3	4	5	( )
27. Gives interesting and stimulating assignments	1	2	3	4	5	( )
28. Gives examinations requiring synthesis of parts of the course	1	2	3	4	5	( )
29. Gives examinations permitting student to show understanding	1	2	3	4	5	( )
30. Keeps students informed of their progress	1	2	3	4	5	( )

Figure 1. *(continued)*

1. Considering both the limitations and possibilities of the subject matter and course, how would you rate the overall teaching effectiveness of this *instructor?*

Not at all effective			*Moderately effective*		*Extremely effective*	
1	2	3	4	5	6	7

2. Focusing now on the course content, how worthwhile was this *course* in comparison with others you have taken at this University?

Not at all worthwhile			*Moderately worthwhile*		*Extremely worthwhile*	
1	2	3	4	5	6	7

3. Are you taking this course because it is required?
   Yes   *No*

Comments:
1. Please use this space to identify what you perceive as the real strengths and weaknesses of:
   a) the course

   b) the instructor's teaching

2. What improvements would you suggest?

Source: Wilson and others (1975).

Figure 2. Sample Teaching Idea—1

File name: 40

If you want to:
Give lectures that are easy to outline
State objectives for each class session
Give students a conceptual framework for taking notes

You may wish to consider:
Giving students a list of questions that covers topics to be addressed in your lecture. One history professor does this routinely. "By outlining my lecture as a series of questions," she explains, "I hope to stimulate the students to think actively during the presentation. The questions are designed to give them a conceptual framework and guide so they can identify where we are and where we are going in the overall discussion.

"I realize that it is difficult for students to listen attentively for a full hour," she says. "Providing them with an outline of the lecture in question format allows them to pick up the thread of the discussion more quickly as their attention fades in and out."

Limitations on Use of Suggestion:

Discipline: None

Course level: None

Course size: None

Mode: Lecture primarily

Conveying Ideas to Other Faculty

In order to pass these ideas along, TECS sent letters of invitation to groups of faculty members asking permission to administer the Student Description of Teaching questionnaire in one of their classes. While the student questionnaire was being administered, the faculty member filled out a Faculty Self-Description of Teaching questionnaire (see Figure 4).

Just before the next time the faculty member taught that same course (usually a year later), a teaching improvement consultation was held. The consultant selected, from the book of ideas compiled as shown in Figures 2 and 3, a half-dozen ideas for each of the faculty member's lowest-rated three or four items.

The topic sentences of these ideas were briefly run past the faculty member, who then selected one or two ideas for each item. Faculty members were asked to select ideas they felt comfortable with and that they felt they might actually be able to put into practice. The consultant described the selected ideas in greater detail, and the written elaborations of the ideas were left with the faculty member.

14

Figure 3. Sample Teaching Idea—2

File name: 145

If you want to:
Have an interesting style of presentation
Capture students' interest

You may wish to consider:
"Opening with gusto" and "finishing strong." Professor Otis Lancaster of the University of Pennsylvania points out the advantages of giving special thought to the beginning and ending of each lecture: "The opening should secure the students' attention and give them the desired 'mental set.' Get off to a good start. Do something to command attention from the outset. Put some punch into your opening.

"Have some form of attention-getter. . . . Some gadget or piece of hardware whose operation depends on the principles of the day's lesson usually excites attention. Carefully planned questions or statements can also develop the curiosity necessary to gain attention. Action is always an attention-getter. If you intend to use charts or models for demonstration materials, have these brought in front of the class after the class is assembled, or keep charts covered until class starts. This will usually whet students' curiosity and make them more eager to see what is going to happen.

"The ending is as important as the beginning. Avoid letting a class session fade into nonexistence. Make an impressive ending. For example, end with: a question or problem—leave it for the class to cogitate and answer before the next meeting; a quotation that conveys the essential theme; a summary—a recapitulation—a miniature review (keep it brief); or what to do before the next class" (Lancaster, 1974, pp. 122-24).

Limitations on Use of Suggestion:

Discipline: None

Course level: None

Course size: None

Mode: Lecture

At the end of the second offering of the class, the new group of students was asked to describe the faculty member's teaching. Mean ratings on the items for which ideas were given were compared for the two occasions. The results of these comparisons are presented in Figure 5 for those items on which ten or more faculty members received suggestions. The results for the item on overall teaching effectiveness are also shown for the forty-six cases for which we had complete data.

As can be seen, the simplest item to change was "states objectives for each class session." Nine out of the ten faculty who were given that suggestion showed a significant positive change.

The hardest item to change was "varies the speed and tone of his/

Figure 4. Faculty Questionnaire

Faculty Self-Description of Teaching

Department _____

Instructor _____ Course Number _____ _____ Quarter, 19_____

I. The following items reflect some of the ways teachers can be described. Please circle the number which indicates the degree to which you feel each item is descriptive of your teaching in this course. In some cases, the statement may not apply. In these cases, check *Doesn't apply/don't know.*

In teaching this course, I:	Not at all descriptive			Very descriptive		Doesn't apply/ don't know
1. Discuss points of view other than my own	1	2	3	4	5	( )
2. Contrast implications of various theories	1	2	3	4	5	( )
3. Discuss recent developments in the field	1	2	3	4	5	( )
4. Give references for more interesting and involved points	1	2	3	4	5	( )
5. Emphasize conceptual understanding	1	2	3	4	5	( )
6. Explain clearly	1	2	3	4	5	( )
7. Am well prepared	1	2	3	4	5	( )
8. Give lectures that are easy to outline	1	2	3	4	5	( )
9. Summarize major points	1	2	3	4	5	( )
10. State objectives for each class session	1	2	3	4	5	( )
11. Identify what I consider important	1	2	3	4	5	( )
12. Encourage class discussion	1	2	3	4	5	( )
13. Invite students to share their knowledge and experience	1	2	3	4	5	( )
14. Invite criticism of my own ideas	1	2	3	4	5	( )
15. Know if the class is understanding me or not	1	2	3	4	5	( )
16. Have students apply concepts to demonstrate understanding	1	2	3	4	5	( )
17. Know when students are bored or confused	1	2	3	4	5	( )
18. Have genuine interest in students	1	2	3	4	5	( )
19. Give personal help to students having difficulties in course	1	2	3	4	5	( )
20. Relate to students as individuals	1	2	3	4	5	( )
21. Am accessible to students out of class	1	2	3	4	5	( )

16

Figure 4. *(continued)*

In teaching this course, I:	Not at all descriptive			Very descriptive		Doesn't apply/ don't know
22. Have an interesting style of presentation	1	2	3	4	5	( )
23. Am enthusiastic about my subject	1	2	3	4	5	( )
24. Vary the speed and tone of my voice	1	2	3	4	5	( )
25. Have interest in and concern for the quality of my teaching	1	2	3	4	5	( )
26. Motivate students to do their best work	1	2	3	4	5	( )
27. Give interesting and stimulating assignments	1	2	3	4	5	( )
28. Give examinations requiring synthesis of parts of the course	1	2	3	4	5	( )
29. Give examinations permitting students to show understanding	1	2	3	4	5	( )
30. Keep students informed of their progress	1	2	3	4	5	( )

II. 1. Prior to this quarter, how many times have you taught this course on the Berkeley campus?

_____ times

2. When do you next expect to teach this course?

_____ Quarter, 19 _____

3. How useful have previous student evaluations of this course been to you in improving:

	Not at all useful		Somewhat useful	Very useful	Doesn't apply
a) the course content or materials	1	2	3	4	5 ( )
b) the assignments or examination	1	2	3	4	5 ( )
c) the course structure, format or organization	1	2	3	4	5 ( )
d) the methods or approaches you use in teaching	1	2	3	4	5 ( )

Figure 4. *(continued)*

4. To what extent do you feel this course could be improved, i.e., how satisfied are you with the course as you taught it this quarter?

   Very dissatisfied, needs improvement   _____

   Somewhat dissatisfied, could be improved   _____

   Generally satisfied, needs little improvement   _____

   Very satisfied, no need to improve at this time   _____

5. How would you rate this class in terms of:

	Very low				Very high
a) your own personal enjoyment	1	2	3	4	5
b) the level of interest shown by the students	1	2	3	4	5
c) the level of performance evidenced by the students	1	2	3	4	5

III. Looking at the items which you rated as not especially descriptive of your teaching in this class, which one(s) would you most like to improve, if any?

Source: Wilson and others (1975).

Figure 5. Statistical Importance of Changes from Time 1 to Time 2

| | Change | | | Total |
Item No.	Decrease	No Change	Increase	Faculty
6. Explains clearly	2 (18%)	3 (27%)	6 (55%)	11
8. Gives lectures that are easy to outline	3 (21%)	2 (14%)	9 (64%)	14
10. States objectives for each class session	1 (10%)	0	9 (90%)	10
12. Encourages class discussion	5 (38%)	2 (15%)	6 (46%)	13
15. Knows if the class understands	8 (25%)	8 (25%)	15 (47%)	32
17. Knows when students are bored	5 (24%)	6 (29%)	10 (48%)	21
22. Has an interesting style of presentation	3 (20%)	3 (20%)	9 (60%)	15
24. Varies the speed and tone of his/her voice	4 (22%)	7 (39%)	7 (39%)	18
26. Motivates students to do their best work	2 (18%)	3 (27%)	6 (55%)	11
30. Keeps students informed of their progress	3 (30%)	1 (10%)	6 (60%)	10
Overall effectiveness of instruction	9 (20%)	13 (28%)	24 (52%)	46

Note: Other items were omitted because fewer than ten clients were given suggestions on those items.

A statistically important change was considered an increase or decrease in mean score from time 1 to time 2 of at least 1/10 of a standard deviation.

Source: Wilson and Tauxe (1986b).

her voice." Only about a third of the eighteen faculty who were given ideas related to this item showed noticeable change.

The item for which the greatest number of faculty were given ideas was "knows if the class is understanding him/her or not." This item is related to the importance of getting feedback from students and is highly correlated with overall effectiveness as a teacher. The greatest number of both faculty clients and their students saw this as an aspect of teaching with which faculty needed help.

Modifying a Successful Procedure

Since 1983, the Council on Educational Development has undertaken additional studies to find less expensive variations of the procedure

Figure 6. Example of Teaching Idea Packet

Teaching Innovation and
Evaluation Services (TIES)
U. C. Berkeley

Teaching Idea Packets (TIPs)
No. 27

Giving Interesting and Stimulating Assignments

The following ideas are suggested and used by faculty members at the University of California, Berkeley.

1. Give a brief early assignment that allows your students to build on knowledge and skills acquired in previous courses.

> One professor of architecture does this in his studio courses. "Beginning with a problem that my students can easily master increases their self-confidence and creates a relaxed, non-threatening atmosphere for the course," he explains. "My first assignment always calls for my students to use skills learned in prior courses and to apply them to an elementary design problem."

2. Give your students at least one assignment that consists of several options.

> One professor of English requires every student to write two essays on assigned topics. His third assignment, however, sets forth five or six options from which his students may choose the one that sounds interesting and most allows them to do their best.
>
> Examples of the options that he offers include: a piece of creative writing; a dramatic representation to be performed in front of the class (which can be a small group or team project); an original videotape to be shown to the class (which can also be a team effort); or a third essay (a "safe" option generally selected by his more conventional students). In addition, with his permission, students can create an option of their own if they wish.
>
> "More than five or six options tends to confuse some students; it becomes too difficult to decide," he believes. "Too few options, on the other hand, restricts unduly my more creative and daring students." Although optional assignments must be related to the subject matter of the course, he encourages his students to take an interdisciplinary approach and to link content and skills from other courses.

3. Give your students the choice of substituting a paper for one of your midterms.

> A professor of classics gives two midterms and one final exam. He has found it useful to give his students the option of writing a paper (from an approved list of topics) for either of the midterms.
>
> "I haven't really noticed any pattern of who takes the midterm and who writes a paper," he comments. "Good and poor students do both. In general about 25 percent of the class chooses to write a paper." He finds that giving his students options increases their motivation and makes them more active learners.

Figure 6. *(continued)*

4. Create opportunities for role playing.

> An engineering professor makes use of role playing to encourage his students to develop skills they will need in their careers. "I give my students copies of an engineering report, for example. Then one half of the class is asked to assume the role of the authors of that report and prepare an oral presentation for the client or funding agency. The other half of the class is assigned to act as representatives of the client or funding agency and to prepare questions to be asked of the engineers.
>
> "About a week later, during class time, I select certain students to actually enact these roles in front of the class. My students do not know ahead of time who will be called upon, so everyone has to be prepared. Those not called on join me in the role of the observer. When the students have enacted the meeting, the rest of us give a critique of each side's performance."

5. Assign provocative or controversial topics for papers.

> "I find that the quality of the papers I get often depends on the quality of the assignment I give," says a professor of business administration. He tries to give provocative topics as paper assignments.
>
> For example, in a recent assignment he asked his students to respond to the question, "If you were working in a company that illegally pollutes the environment what would you do and why?" Giving provocative assignments not only challenges his students and makes for more interesting reading but also diminishes the chance that the papers will be plagiarized.

6. Use a structured process to help your students choose topics and groups.

> In one public health class, students work in small groups on a major project throughout the term. The professor has developed procedures to help his students choose topics and groups. First, all possible project ideas are listed on the board using a brainstorming technique. The question posed to students is "What topics or areas would you like to explore?"
>
> Enough topics are generated so that each is taken on by a group of four to six students. The small groups meet around their selected topic of interest and students explore in detail the nature of their project. At the end of the first period, students indicate on an index card their name, address, phone number, group, and whether their decision is firm. This list is typed and distributed at the next class meeting when needed changes are made.
>
> This procedure gives students a chance to identify appropriate topics and explore in preliminary fashion how they might proceed. It gets students working on their term projects early and has the added benefit of providing each student with a list of everyone in the class and their project interests.

Figure 6. *(continued)*

7. Set up student panels.

> One faculty member in the social sciences organizes the term as a series of student-led discussion. "I believe my students can teach themselves a great deal; therefore I do not play an active role in the student-led discussions. My role is to serve as organizer and facilitator."
>
> In the first week his students select the topic and the date of their presentation. Generally, there are three to four students per topic. Outside class, his students meet as groups with the faculty member to discuss how to organize their topics for presentation and discussion. It is up to each student group to select whatever format they wish for their presentation.
>
> "In the past, student groups have conducted a debate, performed a skit, or simply led a discussion about the topic," he says. "They learn a lot about the topic and they really get to know one another while preparing their presentations."

8. Ask students to analyze an essay or journal article and to write a critique of it.

> One professor of English assigns the work of a literary critic and then asks his students to write an essay taking an adversary position. "If my assignments are provocative," he says, "I get better results. I stress the importance of their presenting a personal point of view. They should enjoy doing the paper; it should provide them with a personal learning experience."
>
> A psychology professor asks his students to write an evaluation or critique of a paper by a professional psychologist. "The process of analysis and evaluation captures what I am trying to do in the course," he explains.

9. Give assignments which put your students in the role of another.

> A history professor reports that she used to give rather standard writing assignments, for example, "compare author X's and Y's views on A," where the two authors tended to be professional historians. "Most undergraduates, however, find the arguments of current historians somewhat arcane," she says.
>
> "Therefore, most recently I have asked my students to read a collection of the eighteenth century speeches on why Louis XVI should be killed and assigned them the task of writing their own speech as if they had been living during the French Revolution.
>
> "Undergraduates really are enthusiastic about this kind of assignment and do an incredibly good job. It helps them to identify with the issues of the time; in fact many of my students went to great lengths to research the authenticity of their own empathic interpretations. Next year, I intend to take this assignment a step further by dividing my students into small groups and having them actually deliver their speeches to the group."

that was associated with success in the Teaching Evaluation Consultation Service. The council identified several essential characteristics of the TECS model for improving faculty teaching:

1. Student evaluations of teaching were used to focus faculty attention on certain facets of their teaching (such as explaining clearly, knowing whether students are understanding, and being accessible).

2. There existed a pool of descriptions of successful teaching practices that were matched to the individual teaching evaluation items.

3. There existed a means (the consultants) for communicating these ideas to faculty at the same time that they received the evaluations of their teaching from a particular class.

Emeritus Consultants. Several of the more recent studies have changed the means used to communicate the descriptions of successful teaching practices to faculty. In one study, sixteen emeritus professors served as teaching consultants, working with thirty-two junior professors and passing along to them the tricks of the trade of teaching. The consultants drew on their own forty years of teaching experience as well as the descriptions of successful teaching practices obtained in the TECS study.

Use of the Compendium of Ideas. One of the outcomes of the Teaching Evaluation Consultation Service was the pool of descriptions of successful teaching practices obtained during interviews with excellent teachers. Over 200 of these ideas were combined into a compendium of suggestions for improving teaching. This compendium served as one of the two final reports of the TECS project. (Wilson and Tauxe, 1986a, 1986b)

The simplest variation to make in efforts to find cost-effective ways to help faculty members change their teaching was to do away with the consultant. What would happen if faculty members were given a summary profile of their teaching in a course and a copy of the compendium of ideas? Could they read the summary (called the Individual Teacher Profiles) of the student evaluations and identify parts of their teaching to change? Could they peruse the compendium of ideas and select some to try out?

To find answers to these questions, we sent twenty-one business administration faculty their Individual Teacher Profiles through the campus mail. They were also sent the compendium of ideas matched with the individual items. They were asked to make changes in those aspects of their teaching that students rated lowest. They were told that the Student Description of Teaching questionnaire was to help them identify what to change; the compendium was to tell them how to change it.

The results were disappointing. Almost half of the group did not use the compendium. Eight faculty reported using one or two ideas. Only two of the twenty-one faculty members used several ideas.

These results point out that if we are going to get faculty to make desired changes in their teaching, we have to get their attention first. For almost half of the experimental group, the experiment was a nonevent. Interviews with faculty suggested that the compendium was too bulky to use easily and efficiently. The Council of Educational Development decided to stop using the compendium and, in its place, developed the Teaching Idea Packets.

Teaching Idea Packets. Teaching Idea Packets (TIPs) are easier for faculty to use in deciding about changes to make in their teaching. A subset of six to ten descriptions of successful teaching practices are included in each TIP (see Figure 6). These were drawn mainly from the original notebooks of teaching ideas. There is a separate TIP to match each item on the Student Description of Teaching questionnaire. Even with the TIPs, however, there was still a need to develop a simple way to get faculty to improve their teaching—a way that was economical of faculty time.

The Berkeley Personal Teaching Guide. The council asked: Would it be possible to develop procedures and/or materials that could combine (1) information from student evaluations of teaching and (2) descriptions of alternative ways of teaching with (3) external intervention (consultation) in selecting possible alternatives? Further, could the results be transmitted to faculty at a time when their motivation to change their teaching would be high?

The Berkeley Personal Teaching Guides (PTGs) were developed as a response to these questions, and their use is currently being studied in several departments. The PTGs are tailored to give individual faculty members Teaching Idea Packets corresponding to the four items students rated as least descriptive of their teaching; these materials are provided with the student ratings at the end of the course. The Personal Teaching Guides includes directions on their construction plus guidelines on how to get started changing one's teaching.

How can we increase the extent of faculty use of these aids to changing their teaching? Will faculty find the Personal Teaching Guide useful enough that they will vote to continue using them? These are the questions currently being asked in our ongoing efforts to encourage improvements in teaching.

References

Davis, B. G., Wood, L., and Wilson, R. C. *ABCs of Teaching with Excellence.* Berkeley: Teaching Innovation and Evaluation Services, University of California, 1983.

Lancaster, O. E. *Effective Teaching and Learning.* New York: Gordon and Breach, 1974.

Wilson, R. C., Gaff, J. G., Dienst, E. R., Wood, L., and Bavry, J. L. *College Professors and Their Impact on Students.* New York: Wiley, 1975.

24

Wilson, R. C., and Tauxe, C. *Faculty Views of Factors That Affect Teaching Excellence in Large Lecture Classes.* Berkeley: Teaching Innovation and Evaluation Services, Research on Teaching Improvement and Evaluation, University of California, 1986a.

Wilson, R. C., and Tauxe, C. *Student Views of Factors That Affect Teaching Excellence in Large Lecture Classes.* Berkeley: Teaching Innovation and Evaluation Services, Research on Teaching Improvement and Evaluation, University of California, 1986b.

Robert C. Wilson is research psychologist and chief of research for the Teaching Innovation and Evaluation Services from 1983 to 1986 at the University of California, Berkeley.

Research shows that typical faculty concerns about student evaluations of instruction are largely unfounded.

Typical Faculty Concerns About Student Evaluation of Teaching

Lawrence M. Aleamoni

Most of the instructional evaluation systems currently in existence consist of only one component—namely, student evaluations. Over the years, I have heard faculty express many concerns about student evaluations or student ratings. This chapter presents eight of the most common concerns and then cites research that reflects on these concerns.

Eight Typical Concerns

The first concern is that students cannot make consistent judgments concerning the instructor and instruction because of their immaturity, lack of experience, and capriciousness.

Second, faculty express a widely held belief that only colleagues with excellent publication records and experience are qualified to evaluate their peers' instruction. In fact, W. Edwards Deming (1972) maintained that such colleagues were the only ones who could qualify as good instructors.

The third typical concern is that most student-rating schemes are nothing more than a popularity contest with the warm, friendly, humorous, easy-grading instructor emerging as the winner every time.

L. M. Aleamoni (ed.). *Techniques for Evaluating and Improving Instruction.*
New Directions for Teaching and Learning, no. 31. San Francisco: Jossey-Bass, Fall 1987.

Fourth, many faculty believe that students are not able to make accurate judgments concerning either instruction or instructor until they have been away from the course, and possibly away from the institution, for several years.

The fifth concern consists of a general indictment of student-rating forms; many faculty members maintain that these forms are both unreliable and invalid.

The sixth concern is that any of several extraneous variables, or conditions, could affect student ratings. Some of these conditions include: the size of the class; the gender of the student; the gender of the instructor; the time of day that the course is offered; whether the students are taking the course as a requirement or as an elective; whether the student is a major or nonmajor in the field; the term or semester that the course is offered; the level of the course (freshman, sophomore, junior, senior, or graduate); and the rank of the teacher, ranging from instructor to full professor.

The seventh concern is that the grades or marks that the students either expect to receive or actually receive are highly related to their ratings of both the course and the instructor. And, finally, faculty members frequently ask how student ratings or evaluations can possibly be used to improve instruction.

What the Research Shows

Now let us consider what the research indicates about each of these concerns. The research dates back over sixty years, especially if we look at Guthrie's (1954) work and his citations dating back to about 1924. In fact, there is a great deal of research literature that addresses these concerns.

First, let us look at whether students are really immature or lack the experience necessary to make consistent judgments. If we examine the research (Guthrie, 1954; Costin, Greenough, and Menges, 1971) and concentrate only on the studies that used reliable and valid instruments, then we find evidence that students' judgments tend to be pretty stable. In fact, some research cited in the *Chronicle of Higher Education* several years ago (Cooper and Petrosky, 1976) pointed out that even students at the secondary level tend to be fairly consistent in what they are saying about instructors and instruction.

Second, Deming's (1972) claim that only colleagues with excellent publication records and experience can, in fact, qualify as good teachers and therefore are the only ones in a position to judge good teaching does not hold up to any reasonable examination. In 1973, a graduate assistant and I (Aleamoni and Yimer, 1973) conducted a fairly comprehensive study at the University of Illinois, tracing the publication records and experiences of the faculty. Because the University of Illinois normally puts out an annual compendium of all faculty publications, we were able to get a pretty accurate estimate of what the faculty had produced. We then asked faculty members themselves to rate the instructional effectiveness of their colleagues in their departments, and we also gathered information from students on the various courses, instructors, and so on. All of these data were correlated. The relationship found between colleague ratings of instructional effectiveness and research productivity, as judged by the number of scholarly publications or by appropriate creative work in the areas of music, art, and so on, was 0.07. The relationship between student ratings and faculty productivity was –0.04. There was no significant difference between the two relationships. Next, we attempted to find the relationship between the colleague rating of instructional effectiveness and the student ratings. This correlation turned out to be quite high: 0.70. The first time this figure was presented to a faculty group, somebody said, "Well, what do you expect? How do you think we learn about so-and-so's teaching. Students come in and sit down and tell us that so-and-so was terrible, so-and-so was great, and so forth. That is where we get the information." We drew on another study (Stallings and Spencer, 1967) to control for that bias. The resulting correlation had the same magnitude— 0.70. These comparisons have been replicated in several other places around the country (Linsky and Straus, 1975; Marsh, 1984).

Third, many studies address the concern that most student ratings are nothing more than a popularity contest. Grush and Costin (1975), for example, looked at students' personal attraction to teachers, compared that attraction to how highly the students rated instructors, and found a very low correlation. Abrami, Leventhal, and Perry (1982), in examining educational seduction and the "Dr. Fox" effect (the influence of instructor personality on student ratings), also maintained that higher ratings could not be attributed simply to the fact that the instructor was providing a nice, friendly, humorous atmosphere in the classroom; the students are much more discriminating than that. In addition, at the University of Illinois, I (Aleamoni, 1976) looked at thousands of subjective written comments from students, compared them to objective ratings, and noted that the students are not easily fooled. In rating their instructors, students discriminate among various aspects of teaching ability: If a teacher tells great jokes and has the students in the palm of his or her hand in the classroom, he or she will receive high ratings in humor and classroom manner, but these ratings do not influence students' assessments of other teaching skills.

The fourth concern—that students cannot make accurate judgments until they have been away from the course or possibly away from the university for several years—was the focus of early studies at Purdue by Drucker and Remmers (1950, 1951). They asked graduates who had been out of the institution for five and ten years to rate the instructors with whom they had studied and who still happened to be at Purdue. Then the researchers asked current students to rate the instructors on the same basic dimensions. Drucker and Remmers found a high positive relationship between the two sets of assessments. In this case the sampling procedure was not ideal because not all alumni responded and the researchers had to rely on whatever data were available. A replication was conducted at the University of Illinois, by asking graduating seniors to look back at their first two years of college (Aleamoni and Yimer, 1974). This procedure was repeated at the University of Washington and the the University of California, Los Angeles, (Marsh, 1977) and resulted in similar findings: a high positive relationship between the judgments made by students who had been away and those made by students who were currently taking the course.

Sheffield (1974) offers extensive evidence of a similar kind. Regarding the fifth concern about the reliability and validity of student-rating forms, it is true that these forms will be unreliable if they have not been professionally constructed and tested. One attribute of a professionally constructed form is that the response scales are anchored; that is, each point on the scale is defined, and numbers are not used in place of adjectives. Undefined points on a scale generate unreliability, and it is true that many scales are still generated in this way today. However, looking at some of the well-established instruments around the country, we can find a number of fairly reliable forms, with reliability of the total instrument measuring 0.90 and above. Examples are the Educational Testing Service (ETS) instrument, Student Instructional Report, the Kansas State instrument, Instructional Development and Effectiveness Assessment, the Arizona Course/Instructor Evaluation Questionnaire, Wilbert McKeachie's items, and Robert Wilson's instrument, Student Description of Teaching. There are also several catalogues (Abrami and Murphy, 1980) of items available to use in constructing reliable instruments.

The validity of student-rating forms, however, is a little tougher issue. If one accepts Deming's (1972) premise that the valid judges are colleagues (or peers), then student-rating forms have a pretty good validity coefficient since they correlate at 0.70 with student judgments. On the other hand, how highly related is student learning to the way students rate? There have been a few studies (Cohen and Berger, 1970; Frey, 1973; Frey, Leonard, and Beatty, 1975; White, Hsu, and Means, 1978) conducted in which objective measures of student learning have been obtained. Generally, those studies have reported a fairly high positive relationship between the objective measures of learning and the way students rate. Again, we have to be careful about the student-rating instruments we use.

Concern number six looks at extraneous variables, eight categories of which were identified. The majority of the research (Aleamoni and Hexner, 1980) I have looked at indicates little or no relationship between such variables as class size, gender of the student or gender of the instructor, the time of day that the class is offered, the major or nonmajor status of the student, or the term or semester that the course is offered and the way in which students rate a course or instructor. The relationship between the rank of the professor and the student ratings is, in some studies, close to being statistically significant, but there really is no pattern in the research that says that, on the whole, full professors are rated more positively than the lecturer or the assistant professor (Aleamoni and Graham, 1974). Interestingly enough, however, when I tried to convince the University of Illinois faculty that such was the case, they said, "We want comparisons by rank." Thus, in our computerized printout of student ratings of faculty, we include a comparison by rank.

The variables that distinguish a required course from an elective and that identify courses by level (freshman, sophomore, and so on) do seem to generate significant differences in student ratings. For example, the higher the proportion of students taking the course as a requirement, the lower the overall rating. Freshmen tend to rate their teachers significantly lower than do sophomores, sophomores tend to rate them significantly lower than do juniors, and so on. A multivariate analysis (Aleamoni and Graham, 1974) was conducted several years ago; the results indicated that the class size or time of day seemed to have a significant effect, but, once one stratified by the level of the course, those effects were no longer significant. So course level should be taken into account when student-rating results are reported.

Many faculty are convinced that the grades or marks the students receive, or expect to receive, are highly related to their ratings. Much research has been conducted in this seventh area of concern. If we plotted the correlations from these studies, we would see a nice bell-shaped curve, where the mean, median, and mode would be close to zero correlation with a standard deviation of approximately 0.16. This should not be surprising, since grades are notoriously unreliable anyway, and they do not necessarily reflect what the student has actually learned.

On the final question of whether student evaluations can possibly be used to improve instruction, we conducted a study (Aleamoni, 1978), repeated by McKeachie and others (1980) at the University of Michigan, that basically demonstrates that, if we provide feedback from a consultant along with the standard computerized output, we will see instructional improvement as a result. A more recent study by Stevens and Aleamoni (1985) provides additional supporting evidence.

Conclusion

What if the tables were turned and the faculty's evaluations of students were being questioned? Let us consider the eight areas of concern from this point of view. How much evidence could we provide to convince students that faculty judgments about their learning are based on solid objective criteria? How much evidence could we provide to convince students that the performance of students with excellent ability is not used to set the standard for the rest of the students in the class? How much evidence could we provide to convince students that most faculty grading schemes are not affected by the attentive, polite, conforming, noncreative student? How much evidence could we provide to convince students that what is taught in the course is useful in other courses, or outside the university? How much evidence could we provide to convince students that the course examinations are both reliable and valid? How much evidence could we provide to convince students that an instructor's marks are not affected by the size of the class, the gender of the student, the time of day that the course is offered, whether the student is taking the course as a requirement or as an elective, whether the student is a major or nonmajor, and so on? How much evidence could we provide to convince students that instructors who had a particularly rough time when they went to college do not tend to be just as rough on their students when they get them in class? And, finally, what evidence could we provide to convince students that course examinations are useful in improving their learning?

References

Abrami, P. C., Leventhal, L., and Perry, R. P. "Educational Seduction." *Review of Educational Research,* 1982, *52* (3), 446–464.

Abrami, P. C., and Murphy, V. A. *Catalogue of Systems for Student Ratings of Instruction.* Montreal, Canada: Centre for Teaching and Learning Services, McGill University, 1980.

Aleamoni, L. M. "Typical Faculty Concerns About Student Evaluation of Instruction." *National Association of Colleges and Teachers of Agriculture Journal,* 1976, *20* (1), 16–21.

Aleamoni, L. M. "The Usefulness of Student Evaluations in Improving College Teaching." *Instructional Science,* 1978, *7,* 95–105.

Aleamoni, L. M., and Graham, M. H. "The Relationship Between CEQ Ratings and Instructor's Rank, Class Size and Course Level." *Journal of Educational Measurement,* 1974, *11,* 189–202.

Aleamoni, L. M., and Hexner, P. Z. "A Review of the Research on Student Evaluation and a Report on the Effect of Different Sets of Instructions on Student Course and Instructor Evaluation." *Instructional Science,* 1980, *9,* 67–84.

Aleamoni, L. M., and Yimer, M. "An Investigation of the Relationship Between Colleague Rating, Student Rating, Research Productivity, and Academic Rank in Rating Instructional Effectiveness." *Journal of Educational Psychology,* 1973, *64,* 274–277.

Aleamoni, L. M., and Yimer, M. *Graduating Senior Ratings' Relationship to Colleague Rating, Student Rating, Research Productivity, and Academic Rank in Rating Instructional Effectiveness.* Research Report No. 352. Urbana: Office of Instructional Resources, Measurement and Research Division, University of Illinois, 1974.

Cohen, S. A., and Berger, W. G. "Dimensions of Students' Ratings of College Instructors Underlying Subsequent Achievement on Course Examinations." *Pro-*

ceedings of the 78th Annual Convention of the American Psychological Association, 1970, *5*, 605–606.

Cooper, C. R., and Petrosky, A. "Secondary School Students' Perceptions of Math Teachers and Math Classes." *Mathematics Teacher*, 1976, *69* (3), 226–233.

Costin, F., Greenough, W. T., and Menges, R. J. "Student Ratings of College Teaching: Reliability, Validity, and Usefulness." *Review of Educational Research*, 1971, *41*, 511–535.

Deming, W. E. "Memorandum on Teaching." *American Statistician*, 1972, *26*, 47.

Drucker, A. J., and Remmers, H. H. "Do Alumni and Students Differ in Their Attitudes Toward Instructors?" *Purdue University Studies in Higher Education*, 1950, *70*, 62–64.

Drucker, A. J., and Remmers, H. H. "Do Alumni and Students Differ in Their Attitudes Toward Instructors?" *Journal of Educational Psychology*, 1951, *42*, 129–143.

Frey, P. W. "Student Ratings of Teaching: Validity of Several Rating Factors." *Science*, 1973, *182*, 83–85.

Frey, P. W., Leonard, D. W., and Beatty, W. W. "Student Ratings of Instruction: Validation Research." *American Educational Research Journal*, 1975, *12* (4), 435–447.

Grush, J. E., and Costin, F. "The Student as Consumer of the Teaching Process." *American Educational Research Journal*, 1975, *12*, 55–66.

Guthrie, E. R. *The Evaluation of Teaching: A Progress Report*. Seattle: University of Washington, 1954.

Linsky, A. S., and Straus, M. A. "Student Evaluations, Research Productivity, and Eminence of College Faculty." *Journal of Higher Education*, 1975, *46*, 89–102.

McKeachie, W. J., Lin, Y-G., Daugherty, M., Moffett, M., Neigler, C., Nork, J., Walz, M., and Baldwin, R. "Using Student Ratings and Consultation to Improve Instruction." *British Journal of Educational Psychology*, 1980, *50*, 168–174.

Marsh, H. W. "The Validity of Students' Evaluations: Classroom Evaluations of Instructors Independently Nominated as Best and Worst Teachers by Graduating Seniors." *American Educational Research Journal*, 1977, *14*, 441–447.

Marsh, H. W. "Students' Evaluations of University Teaching: Dimensionality, Reliability, Validity, Potential Biases, and Utility." *Journal of Educational Psychology*, 1984, *76* (5), 707–754.

Sheffield, E. F. (ed.). *Teaching in the Universities: No One Way*. Montreal, Canada: McGill-Queen's University Press, 1974.

Stallings, W. M., and Spencer, R. E. *Ratings of Instructors in Accountancy 101 from Videotape Clips*. Research Report No. 265. Urbana: Office of Instructional Resources, Measurement and Research Division, University of Illinois, 1967.

Stevens, J. J., and Aleamoni, L. M. "The Use of Evaluative Feedback for Instructional Improvement: A Longitudinal Perspective." *Instructional Science*, 1985, *13*, 285–304.

White, W. F., Hsu, Y. M., and Means, R. S. "Prediction of Student Ratings of College Instructors from Multiple Achievement Test Variables." *Educational and Psychological Measurement*, 1978, *38* (4), 1077–1083.

*Lawrence M. Aleamoni is professor of educational psychology
and director of the Office of Instructional Research and
Development at the University of Arizona.*

Instructional improvement programs are most likely to be effective when a more complete model is used.

Using Student Ratings to Improve Instruction

Joseph J. Stevens

The use of student ratings as a method of course and instructor evaluation has increased substantially over the past ten years. With this increase, a number of standardized instruments for assessing instructional effectiveness have become available. These instruments provide a reliable and relatively simple methodology for obtaining student evaluations of instruction. Recent reviews of the validity of student ratings have tended to support their usefulness as a measure of instructional effectiveness (Aleamoni, 1980; Aleamoni and Hexner, 1980; Centra, 1979; Cohen, 1980; Kulik and Kulik, 1974; Marsh, 1980; McKeachie, 1979; Millman, 1981). Information derived from student evaluations, however, may serve a number of purposes. Cohen (1980) defined three such purposes: (1) to aid in administrative decisions, (2) to aid students in course or instructor selection, and (3) to provide feedback to instructors for instructional improvement.

     This last purpose of student evaluations, that of instructional improvement, is the focus of this chapter. Some disagreement exists in recent reviews regarding the effectiveness of student evaluations for improving instruction. A review by Rotem and Glasman (1979) concluded that "feedback from student ratings . . . does not seem to be effective for the purpose of improving performance of university teachers" (p. 507). However, a number of studies have found substantial increases in student rat-

L. M. Aleamoni (ed.). *Techniques for Evaluating and Improving Instruction.*
New Directions for Teaching and Learning, no. 31. San Francisco: Jossey-Bass, Fall 1987.

ings as a function of feedback to the instructor. And, in at least one study (Overall and Marsh, 1979), feedback to the instructor produced subsequent gains not only in student ratings but also in student motivation and achievement.

The effectiveness of student evaluations for instructional improvement was reviewed most recently by Cohen (1980). Cohen conducted a meta-analysis of instructional feedback studies and concluded that student-ratings feedback had a modest but significant effect (15 percentile points) in improving instruction. Cohen also found that this effect was accentuated when consultation accompanied feedback. In a recent study, Stevens and Aleamoni (1985) found that instructors who received student-ratings feedback with consultation maintained higher student ratings over a ten-year period than instructors who received student-ratings feedback alone.

Thus, the research literature reports inconsistent results when student ratings are used to provide feedback for instructional improvement. On the other hand, logically, one would not assume that the provision of evaluative feedback alone would necessarily result in consistent instructional improvement; the results reported in the literature, therefore, should not be surprising. The discrepancies in these results might be attributed to methodological differences in how feedback is provided and to the interaction of instructor characteristics with the feedback methodology. Thus, we need to determine how to maximize the effects of feedback for instructional improvement and how to identify factors that either constrain or facilitate improvement.

Factors Influencing Instructional Improvement

A number of authors have specified factors that may be responsible for failures of instructor improvement following student-ratings feedback (Cohen, 1980; Kulik and Kulik, 1974; McKeachie, 1979). I have incorporated these factors here, along with several additional ones, in an illustrative model of instructional improvement. First, we must consider that the cognitive state of the instructor is influenced by an array of external and internal conditions (Figure 1). Both the desire and the ability of the instructor to change at a given point in time will be a function of instructor motivation, attitudes, and knowledge (at the least). The effectiveness of providing feedback for instructional improvement is dependent on conditions that allow feedback information to be received favorably and, once received, to be applied as part of a meaningful strategy for change.

Let us now consider in greater detail the external and internal conditions that can directly or indirectly influence the effectiveness of feedback information. Instructional behavior obviously is influenced by a wealth of external factors. Different agents can exert influence over the instructor and thereby affect the individual's instructional behavior. These agents

Figure 1. Influences on the Cognitive State of the Instructor

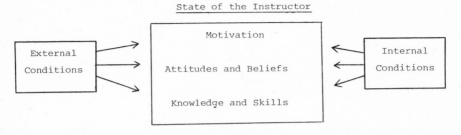

would include the institution, the instructor's colleagues, and the instructor's students. Each of these agents is likely to have some impact on all three aspects of the instructor's cognitive state as diagrammed in Figure 1. For example, instructor motivation is directly influenced by the institutional incentives and rewards (such as promotion, merit increases, awards, and so on) that are offered for instruction or instructional improvement. And an instructor's attitudes and beliefs about instruction and instructional behavior might be influenced by the opinions, behavior, and proscriptions of close colleagues.

Similarly, internal factors may influence greatly the way in which feedback information is received and used by the instructor. The instructor may not be motivated to change for a variety of reasons, or the instructor may not believe change is possible or even desirable. This attitudinal constraint on instructional improvement is commonly evidenced by the questionable assertion that "good teachers are born, not made." Last, and perhaps most important, the instructor may not possess adequate skills and knowledge to understand, interpret, and apply feedback information. For example, the instructor may be wholly unaware of alternative methods of instruction, course preparation, or methods for effecting change. In this case, although feedback information may be understood, the instructor is incapable of applying the information. Since few institutions provide explicit training on instructional methods as part of their graduate programs, we can reasonably assume that a large portion of college and university instructors, at some point in their careers, are deficient to some degree in the skills necessary for effective instruction or for effecting instructional improvement.

The current cognitive state of an instructor, then, will vary greatly from one individual to another, and, as a result, the manner in which feedback information is received by the instructor will also vary greatly. For example, if an instructor tends to doubt the validity of student evaluations and receives feedback that is inconsistent with his or her self-evaluation, then he or she is likely to discount the value of student feedback and is unlikely to change. A second hypothetical instructor might possess the internal motivation, attitudes, and skills to make changes but be subject to external constraints (such as lack of time or lack of instructional resources) that prevent or delay these changes. Since the majority of instructional intervention studies occur over a period of less than one semester (Stevens and Aleamoni, 1985), such delayed changes are difficult to detect.

Student Ratings as One Element in a Complete System

Thus, on closer examination, we can see that the provision of student-ratings feedback to the instructor is an incomplete tactic for producing instructional improvement. This contention is supported by the inconsistency of improvement in feedback studies. However, this view does not necessarily argue against the utility of student ratings for instructional improvement; rather, it is more likely that the reported results demonstrate the complexity of the instructional milieu (as illustrated above) and the inadequacy of the "treatment" design of instructional intervention studies.

The more promising results reported for studies using feedback in combination with consultation are also consistent with the model presented here. Interaction between the instructor and the consultant provides an opportunity to address the instructor's motivation, attitude, and knowledge as part of the process of instructional improvement. Although most studies have not reported or controlled experimentally the specific components of consultation, such consultation has, at the least, probably improved the instructor's ability to interpret feedback information. Controlled studies that address these different cognitive factors or that examine different types of supplemental consultation have yet to occur.

Student-ratings feedback is therefore best viewed as one means of gathering information for instructional improvement. Student-ratings instruments, when properly developed, provide the most reliable and cost-efficient means of obtaining feedback, but they are best supplemented by additional sources of evaluative information (such as peers, administrators, and so on). Any feedback, however, is unlikely to produce meaningful instructional improvement without the recognition that obtaining evaluative information is only the first step in a larger process, as shown in Figure 2. In this diagram, evaluation leads to the identification of areas of concern or interest that the instructor wishes to improve. As a result of

Figure 2. The Process Involved in Instructional Change

EVALUATION ⟶ IDENTIFICATION ⟶ DESIGN ⟶ IMPLEMENTATION

identification, tactics for change are designed and implemented. Evaluation then occurs to assess the effectiveness of the instructional changes made. Feedback is critical to the successful completion of the first steps in this diagram and to the evaluation of the success of new instructional plans or methods. The remainder of this process, however, is dependent on the application of additional information, skills, and resources. Studies that endeavor to use only feedback for instructional improvement have, therefore, adopted a truncated or simplistic view of this process. When we assume that feedback information, in and of itself, leads to instructional improvement, the actual needs of the instructor may be neglected.

Summary

The research literature reports that student-ratings feedback is inconsistent in producing instructional improvement. These results are easily reconciled by a subjective model that assumes that instructor change requires more than evaluative information. This model assumes that several aspects of the instructor's cognitive state (motivation, attitude, and knowledge) are directly responsible for the manner in which evaluative information is received and, once received, for the manner in which it is applied or ignored. Evaluation, then, is only one part of a larger improvement process. Successful improvement of the instructor requires the support of the cognitive needs of the instructor at several stages in this process.

The view presented here is that studies of instructional improvement have adopted an unnecessarily simplistic approach that is unlikely to produce consistent gains for instructors. Simply providing feedback is an insufficient tactic for behavioral change in a milieu as complex as the college or university teaching environment. Although some instructors will react positively to feedback and be able to monitor their own improvement as a result, most instructors can be presumed to have deficiencies in one or several aspects of the cognitive model presented above. These deficiencies are likely to hamper or prevent instructional improvement.

Instructional improvement programs are most likely to be effective when a more complete model of instructional improvement is used. This suggests the use of reliable but flexible methods for providing feedback information to the instructor. However, it also suggests a system of institutional support, reward, and training for instructional improvement. The instructor must often be educated in how to conceptualize, interpret, and apply feedback information. Additionally, the instructor must learn how to design and implement alternative instructional procedures in response to feedback, which means that a coherent system of instructional resources must be easily available to the instructor. Without such a system, the instructor may be unable to gain the knowledge or support that is necessary to effect change. When this is the case, then student-ratings feed-

38

back, at the most, can be expected to produce inconsistent and incomplete instructional improvement.

References

Aleamoni, L. M. "The Use of Student Evaluations in the Improvement of Instruction." *National Association of Colleges and Teachers of Agriculture*, 1980, *24* (3), 18–21.

Aleamoni, L. M., and Hexner, P. Z. "A Review of the Research on Student Evaluation and a Report on the Effect of Different Sets of Instructions on Student Course and Instructor Evaluation." *Instructional Science*, 1980, *9*, 67–84.

Centra, J. A. *Determining Faculty Effectiveness: Assessing Teaching, Research, and Service for Personnel Decisions and Improvements.* San Francisco: Jossey-Bass, 1979.

Cohen, P. A. "Effectiveness of Student-Rating Feedback for Improving College Instruction: A Meta-Analysis of Findings." *Research in Higher Education*, 1980, *13* (4), 321–341.

Cohen, P. A. "Student Ratings of Instruction and Student Achievement: A Meta-Analysis of Multisection Validity Studies." *Review of Educational Research*, 1981, *51*, 281–309.

Kulik, J. A., and Kulik, C.L.C. "Student Ratings of Instruction." *Teaching of Psychology*, 1974, *1*, 51–57.

McKeachie, W. J. "Student Ratings of Faculty: A Reprise." *Academe*, 1979, *65*, 384–397.

Marsh, H. W. "Research on Students' Evaluations of Teaching Effectiveness: A Reply to Vecchio." *Instructional Evaluation*, 1980, *4*, 5–13.

Millman, J. (ed.). *Handbook of Teacher Evaluation.* Beverly Hills, Calif.: Sage, 1981.

Overall, J. U., and Marsh, H. W. "Midterm Feedback from Students: Its Relationship to Instructional Improvement and Students' Cognitive and Affective Outcomes." *Journal of Educational Psychology*, 1979, *71*, 856–865.

Rotem, A., and Glasman, N. S. "On the Effectiveness of Students' Evaluative Feedback to University Instructors." *Review of Educational Research*, 1979, *49*, 497–511.

Stevens, J. J., and Aleamoni, L. M. "The Use of Evaluative Feedback for Instructional Improvement: A Longitudinal Perspective." *Instructional Science*, 1985, *13*, 285–304.

Joseph J. Stevens is research associate in the Office of Instructional Research and Development and adjunct professor of psychology at the University of Arizona.

Student governments have valuable roles to play in comprehensive faculty evaluation programs.

The Role of Student Government in Faculty Evaluation

Raoul A. Arreola

During the last dozen or so years that I have spent designing or operating faculty evaluation systems around the country, student governments have rarely played a serious role. However, a number of major student-rating systems had their beginnings as student government efforts. The fact that student governments have not continued to play major roles in the faculty evaluation efforts of colleges and universities, in spite of the fact that these governments were instrumental, in many cases, in getting student-rating programs started, leads to the question that is the focus of this chapter: What *ought* to be the role of student governments today in a comprehensive faculty evaluation program?

Historical Perspective

Student ratings were developed many years ago, often at the instigation of student governments and other student groups, primarily to provide students with a guide as to which faculty's courses to take and which to avoid. In a sense, this application of student ratings represented the essence of faculty evaluation, since it meant that students could "vote

L. M. Aleamoni (ed.). *Techniques for Evaluating and Improving Instruction.*
New Directions for Teaching and Learning, no. 31. San Francisco: Jossey-Bass, Fall 1987.

with their feet"—or perhaps more correctly, with their registration fees—in reflecting their collective evaluation of the worth of an instructor. Early student ratings, therefore, were designed to help students select "good" faculty and avoid "bad" ones.

Student-rating questionnaires designed by student governments often asked such questions as "What grade would you give this instructor?" or, more germane to the purpose of the ratings, "Would you recommend this instructor to a friend?" The ratings of faculty would then be published and distributed or sold to the general student body to be used as registration guides.

To a certain degree, such publications were successful, and a few such documents persist to this day. However, it was often found that students could not always sign up to take the highly rated instructors or could not always avoid the poorly rated ones for a number of bureaucratic and scheduling reasons. In any case, since faculty could not be required to participate in such student endeavors, only faculty volunteers would appear in the publications. Naturally, very few faculty who consistently received poor ratings would volunteer for such exposure. As a consequence, rating systems that were designed and administered by student governments never became quite the faculty evaluation programs that students had dreamed they would be.

In addition, because the interest among students in supporting student governments and their activities is mercurial at best, it often happened that, after a student-rating system had been established and had operated for a while, the student government would either lose interest, run out of money, or both. At that point, the university administration would step in and take it over; thus was born the university's so-called student evaluation programs.

Student Evaluation, Student Ratings, and Faculty Evaluation

Before examining what current role student governments ought to play in a faculty evaluation program, we should first distinguish among the terms *student evaluation, student ratings,* and *faculty evaluation.*

The term *student evaluation* seems to have evolved from the combining of the terms *student ratings* and *faculty evaluation.* In fact, many faculty and administrators have ceased to discriminate between the two terms and simply talk about student evaluation of faculty. Faculty evaluation, however, is actually an assignment carried out for the purpose of making a decision concerning promotion, tenure, or merit pay; students do not engage directly in faculty evaluation when they respond to a rating form.

On the other hand, most student-rating forms simply gather information concerning student opinions, reactions, and observations about the course and the instructor. These ratings are then utilized in one of two ways: They may be used by the instructor for self-evaluation and self-improvement purposes, or they may be used by decision makers, in conjunction with other evidence, as the basis for arriving at a personnel decision. In essence, therefore, student ratings are either a form of feedback to the instructor about his or her classroom performance or but one piece of a mosaic that is put together to describe the overall performance of an instructor for administrative decision-making purposes. In the first instance, the faculty member is the evaluator, and in the second an administrator or some peer group performs the evaluation. In either case, students do not evaluate faculty in the sense of gathering data and making a personnel decision. Thus, we should stop talking about student evaluation and instead refer to student ratings, which may be a part of an overall faculty evaluation system.

Role of Students in Faculty Evaluation

Some form of faculty evaluation has always existed in colleges and universities. It may have taken the form of something as formal as a peer review procedure with administrative guidance, or it may have been something as informal as the department chair or dean deciding who was to get what rewards.

In addition, students have always had a role in that faculty evaluation process, although it may not always have been structured or organized. I recall working with one college in the establishment of a formal faculty evaluation program that employed student ratings. The faculty of the college were very critical of the general validity of student-rating forms and argued that they should not be used until they had been "proved." The dean of the college took me aside and told me that, regardless of what the faculty said, he would welcome any form of student ratings. When I asked why, the dean said that, although he was ashamed to admit it, there were times when the only information he had on which he could base his evaluation of a faculty member was hearsay from an embarrassingly few students.

I often think about that situation when I hear faculty criticisms about the validity of student-rating forms. Whether we like it or not, students have had, and will continue to have, input to decision makers concerning the evaluation of faculty. The question, then, is: What is the best way to structure and organize that input so that it is accurate, relevant, and placed in the proper perspective. What elements of faculty performance ought to be evaluated, and which sources of information are most appropriate and credible for each element?

One of the critical steps in designing a comprehensive faculty evaluation program is to develop a role-by-source matrix (see Figure 1). In such a matrix, one first designates the elements to be evaluated; in this

Figure 1. A Role-by-Source Matrix

ROLE   SOURCES

TEACHING	STUDENTS	PEERS	SELF	DEPT. CHAIR
Instructional Delivery Skills	YES	NO	YES	NO
Instructional Design Skills	YES	YES	YES	NO
Content Expertise	NO	YES	YES	YES
Record Keeping/ Management	NO	NO	YES	YES

Source: Arreola (1979).

example, teaching is broken down into four major elements: instructional delivery skills, instructional design skills, content expertise, and record keeping/management. Then the possible sources of information for each of these elements are identified.

Generally, speaking, students are appropriate sources of information for what goes on in the classroom. That is, we can ask students to serve as observers of a faculty member's instructional delivery skills. Through appropriately designed questionnaires, we can solicit from them their observations concerning the description of certain characteristics, the occurrence or nonoccurrence of certain events, and the frequency of occurrence of others. Additionally, students are the best sources concerning their own opinions and reactions to classroom teaching events and supporting materials prepared by the faculty member that reflect his or her instructional design skills.

We must then prepare such matrices for each of the various roles faculty play that may be included in a comprehensive faculty evaluation program. Such roles include: advising, publishing articles or books, teaching, research, faculty or college service, participation in professional organizations, administration and management, professional development, and community service.

From these matrices, we can begin to get a clear picture of the role students may legitimately fill in a faculty evaluation program. The majority of student input will come from ratings concerning teaching, advising, and student group sponsorship. Of these the most substantial student input concerns teaching. With this understanding, let me now turn to the role of student governments in faculty evaluation.

Student Government Roles

By using the term *faculty evaluation program*, I assume that the program includes sources of input from peers, self, and administrators in addition to student ratings. There are, however, a number of faculty evaluation programs in existence that do disservice to the faculty, the students, and the administrators by utilizing student ratings as their sole formally recognized source of information. Such systems may provide good information on which to base the evaluation of a faculty member's instructional delivery skills, and they may provide useful feedback to the instructor for self-improvement purposes, but they do not constitute a complete faculty evaluation program.

In a comprehensive evaluation program, student input can and should play a valuable role (Aleamoni, 1976); however, the value of student input is largely dependent on how credible it is with both the faculty and the administration. Interestingly, the quality of student input, on which its credibility is based, is a function not only of the reliability and appropriateness of the questionnaires or rating forms used to gather that input but also of the degree to which students believe that their input will count. That is, the believability of student ratings on the part of faculty is a direct function of the believability of the faculty and administration on the part of students. If students do not believe that their input will be taken seriously and that it will have some impact on the decision-making process, then the information they provide is likely to be of little value. Likewise, if students do not trust the administrators of a student-rating program to keep their ratings anonymous, they will not give any negative ratings for fear of retribution by the teacher.

In talking with various student governments and other student groups around the country about student ratings, I have found the following statements to represent their paramount concerns: "Why bother to fill out a rating form? Everybody knows they just throw them away." Or, "I wouldn't dare give a professor a bad rating or write anything on the back because he might recognize my handwriting and knock my grade down."

It is the establishment and maintenance of the joint credibility of students with faculty and faculty with students that are the main roles student governments should be playing in a faculty evaluation program. In maintaining this joint credibility, student governments are, in essence, assuring the continued validity of student ratings—assuming, of course, that the student-rating forms have been constructed and administered correctly.

As I noted earlier, the interest and strength of student government groups in any one issue or activity may vary considerably from year to year. Generally, each new student government has to be treated as if no previous student government had existed. We cannot count on student governments taking an aggressive, self-initiated role in a faculty evaluation program; rather, the administration running the program should consider student governments primarily as one important tool in maintaining the validity of one segment of the faculty evaluation effort. With this being the case, I can offer the following guidelines to faculty and administrative groups responsible for operating a faculty evaluation program:

1. Treat every student government group as if it were the first one your institution has ever had. Assume no history and no prior knowledge about faculty evaluation and student-rating programs, even though there may have been a working relationship with the student government for years. Student governments are forever new.

2. In order to establish the credibility of the faculty and the administration with the students, consider having a representative of the student government sit on the faculty evaluation committee. Perhaps you should even let them sit in on the segments of promotion and tenure meetings where the student input is being considered.

3. Work with student government leaders in preparing and issuing a press release every term that the student ratings are administered. This press release should appear in the student paper and make the following points:

a. Student ratings are actually used in the faculty evaluation program; what students say can have an effect on the career of an instructor.

b. The faculty evaluation system is designed so that faculty will not see student ratings before grades are issued. Also, student anonymity is maintained even when the forms are returned to the instructor.

c. Students should fill out all questionnaires accurately and fairly. This is their chance to have their say.

d. There should be a detailed description of the correct method by which the student-rating forms should be administered. For example, the standard directions to be read by the administrator of the rating forms should be printed, it should be made clear that the instructor is not to be circulating in the room while the students are filling in the forms, and so on.

e. There should be a brief explanation of the entire faculty evaluation program with a clear indication of the role and impact student ratings have in the program.

4. If possible, utilize student government manpower to accomplish the following tasks:

a. Administer the student-rating forms. This is not always practical, especially in a large institution that administers forms to all classes each term.

b. Type up the written comments that appear on the backs of the student-rating forms. This is done to alleviate student fears that their handwriting will be recognized. This, too, may not be practical in large institutions.

c. Conduct an annual student survey to assess student concerns or suggestions relating to the rating system or the faculty evaluation program as a whole.

5. Last but not least, pay special attention to student attitudes toward their student government. Occasionally a student government will be installed that represents only a minority of the general student body and has little or no credibility. Taking some of the actions suggested above with such a student government can sometimes result in further undermining their credibility since they will be seen as having "sold out" to the university administration. This can only harm your overall faculty evaluation program. It is better in such situations simply to down-play your interaction with the student government that year and wait for another group to come along.

Conclusion

In some institutions that have a long history of strong and effective student governments, such organizations can play an extremely valuable role in establishing and maintaining the validity of the student-rating component. However, at best, particular students within a student government will be around for only four years. Generally, student governments change rather substantially every year or so, while the faculty and the administration are likely to remain with the institution for a considerable length of time. It is, ultimately, the interaction of the latter two groups that is the major factor in the success or failure of a faculty evaluation program; students are, of course, the third major element in the equation that must always be taken into account. Student governments can play a valuable role in our faculty evaluation programs only when they provide faculty and administrators with a clear and open channel of communication with that third element.

References

Aleamoni, L. M. "Proposed System for Rewarding and Improving Instructional Effectiveness." College and University, 1976, 51, 330–338.

Arreola, R. A. "Strategy for Developing a Comprehensive Faculty Evaluation System." Engineering Education, December 1979, 239–244.

Raoul A. Arreola is professor and chair of the Department of Education at the Center for the Health Sciences, the University of Tennessee, Memphis.

A variety of evaluation methods and their uses are discussed.

Formative and Summative Evaluation: Parody or Paradox?

John A. Centra

Titles are sometimes the only thing that people remember about what they read. This conclusion was reached about ten years ago at the first of these conferences on student ratings and faculty evaluation at Temple University. I used the title "The Student as Godfather" and talked about the impact of student ratings on academia. People remembered the title but not much of what was said. Perhaps a more memorable title for this chapter would be "The Joy of Evaluating Teaching." Or, taking the notion a step farther, maybe some subtitles should be included that would fix in the reader's memory important parts of the content. So, using variations of movie titles, I could add the subtitle "Ordinary Ratings" to stress that student ratings provide only one view of teaching and that we must be wary of their limitations. Another subtitle might be "The Faculty Strikes Back" to suggest that faculty have often felt that they should play a larger role in evaluating their colleagues. A third subtitle might be "Close Encounters of the Worst Kind," implying that there are problems with ratings based on classroom visitations when such information is used for personnel decisions. The fourth subtitle could be lifted from the original movie without variation: "Raging Bull." It would reflect the absurdity of

L. M. Aleamoni (ed.). *Techniques for Evaluating and Improving Instruction.*
New Directions for Teaching and Learning, no. 31. San Francisco: Jossey-Bass, Fall 1987.

self-ratings when people know that such ratings will be used in personnel decisions. A fifth theme might be captured in the subtitle "Whose Ratings Are They Anyway?"—the feeling that many faculty members have that student ratings should be kept confidential. And, finally, "Deep Threat" would focus on the many faculty members who feel threatened by any kind of evaluation.

In fact, this chapter addresses six topics that are related to these suggested subtitles. Four of the topics are frequently discussed: student ratings, colleague evaluation, the issue of what is good teaching, and the issue of whether teacher-designed examinations should be used as a measure of teaching. A fifth topic is something that is too little addressed: the evaluation of research scholarship. And I conclude with some comments on the politics of evaluation.

Student Ratings

A few people, such as Remmers (1949) at Purdue and Guthrie (1954) at the University of Washington, researched student ratings in the thirties and forties: At that time, the ratings were used pretty much on a voluntary basis. In recent years, student ratings have become required at most institutions, and their use has shifted from the formative, which encourages instructional development, to the summative where they play an important role in personnel decisions.

Faculty members can quickly give a number of reasons for this shift: First, retrenchment is going on, and much more discriminating decisions about who gets tenure must be made. There is also more emphasis on merit raises now that budgets are being cut or are not being increased as much. And there is certainly more emphasis on the legal aspects of evaluation, so students' ratings become a way of getting some kind of "objective evidence" into a teacher's file.

Recent research (Millman, 1981) has shed new light on the validity of student ratings and on what these ratings really mean. Do they really reflect how good a teacher is, for example, or are they reflecting the teacher's personality, entertainment skills, or any of several extraneous factors not associated with teaching?

Many studies (Aleamoni and Hexner, 1980; McKeachie, 1979; Marsh, 1984) in the last ten years have looked at the validity of student ratings by comparing the ratings to how much students learn from a particular professor. These studies have been designed for lower-level courses where ten or twenty instructors teach a specific course, such as introductory psychology or freshman English, where there is a common final exam, and where students are assigned to instructors on a random basis. (Ideally, the instructors should not even make up the final exam; it should be made up by other members of the department.) Such studies have found that student ratings are reasonably correlated with student learning. One of McKeachie's students, Peter Cohen (1981), did a meta-analysis of these studies and concluded that the correlations were about 0.50, using the global rating. Some diagnostic items correlated much less with learning, however, and that is a critical point: It means that the global items should be particularly important for summative evaluation. As McKeachie (1979) has pointed out, we really cannot be sure to what extent these findings will generalize to upper-level courses or to courses where only one or two teachers are teaching a section. But this sort of evidence has certainly helped in both the summative and formative uses of student ratings.

Another question is one that is much discussed by those interested in faculty development: Have the ratings really been all that useful in improving instruction? Studies (Aleamoni, 1978, Braunstein, Klein, and Pachla, 1973, Centra, 1973, Miller, 1971) have shown modest changes in teaching, particularly for instructors who are using ratings for the first time. But what happens when these ratings are used time after time? Is there a point of diminishing returns if the same form is used term after term? My guess is that their formative impact diminishes considerably and that the ratings are then used only for personnel decisions, if at all.

Colleague Evaluations

My impression is that faculty peer ratings are made largely to faculty personnel committees. In some instances, senior faculty members consult with department heads, but there is no evidence that, even when given the opportunity, faculty members generally want to visit each other's classes for the purposes of evaluation. Faculty do not want to take the time to do so, and they also see such visitations as promoting adversarial relationships that they do not think are beneficial.

At Carnegie-Mellon some years ago (Centra, 1975), a considerable effort was made to get all faculty involved in visiting and rating one another. It did not work. In fact, the final outcome was that the faculty endorsed student ratings rather than continuing the visitations program.

A similar experience occurred at a university in Florida (Centra, 1975) that wanted to set up an evaluation system that would involve not only student ratings but also faculty visitations. The administrators set up a program where each faculty member would be visited twice by three colleagues. The colleagues filled out rating forms and sent them to me in order to maintain confidentiality. My task was then to analyze the data. These ratings turned out to be very biased: 94 percent of the faculty was rated excellent or good. In addition, the faculty did not like the program and voted not to continue it. They did encourage visitations on an informal basis, but they did not want to write down any evaluations of each other.

Tony Grasha (1977) of the University of Cincinnati developed the notion of peer triads, where three faculty members get together and share materials and objectives, visit each other's classes, and then make suggestions to each other. It's a nice idea, but, other than at Cincinnati, it has yet to catch on elsewhere.

Definitions of Good Teaching

Surveys (Wotruba and Wright, 1974) of faculty members, students, and administrators, in which the question "What are characteristics of good teachers?" was asked, have resulted in the following list of nine characteristics: communication skills, favorable attitudes toward students, knowledge of subject, good organization of subject matter and course, enthusiasm about subject, fairness in examinations and grading, willingness to experiment, encouragement of students to think, and good speaking ability. As we look through the list, it is apparent that many of these same characteristics are on most student-rating forms and peer departmental rating forms. Once they are a part of these ratings forms, people sometimes conclude that a good teacher has to be good in *everything* on that list or everything on the rating form, not taking into account that there are different teaching styles. A good teacher certainly has some of the characteristics on the list, but there would be very few people who would exhibit every one of them. There are some colleges where, unfortunately, administrators simply take a sum total of ratings on the variety of characteristics as a way of evaluating a person's overall teaching.

What might be another way of looking at good teaching? I could argue that good teaching occurs when the instructor uses a method that is best suited to his or her abilities and also best suited to accomplishing what the course should accomplish. If we look at the various methods presented in Figure 1, we realize that not every teacher will be good at all of them. Not everyone, for example can be a dynamic lecturer, yet that is what most teachers do. Even if they are fairly good as lecturers, after twenty years of doing it they may become stale. In other words, it makes sense to encourage a variety of methods in such a way that teachers know they are not going to jeopardize their evaluation by trying something new.

It is equally obvious that no single method is best for all outcomes of instruction. A lecture or film is certainly excellent for transmitting knowledge but not for developing creativity; it is not as good as other methods for developing independent thinking or job skills either. The characteristics listed toward the top of Figure 1 are going to be better at fostering those kinds of outcomes. Simulation and gaming, for example, are ways to involve students directly and enable them to learn important concepts through experience. Thus, the continuum of instructional methods shown in Figure 1 moves from the top, where there is more instructor

Figure 1. Instructional Methods:
Ratio of Teacher Activity Level to Student Activity Level

High   Lecture, Films, Slides

↑   Lecture/Discussion, Questioning, Socratic Method

Seminars, Case Method

Simulating and Gaming, Role Playing, Debating

Individualized Instruction:
 • Personalized System of Instruction (PSI)
 • Audio-Tutorial
 • Computer-Assisted Instruction

Supervised Independent Study Labs, Tutorial

↓   Independent Study (Unsupervised), Student Research,
Low   Independent Field Work

activity and students are passive, to the bottom, where students become more active and the instructor becomes more of a manager of learning.

In short, faculty evaluation should be encouraging teachers to use a variety of methods depending on what they want students to learn. And, if a rating form is causing teachers to continue lecturing when they do not think that is most appropriate, then this problem in the evaluation system needs to be addressed.

Teacher-Designed Examinations

Speaking of outcomes leads to the next topic, which is the influence of tests on teaching and learning. Norman Fredericksen (1984) a former director of research at the Educational Testing Service (ETS), points to strong evidence that tests influence both teacher and student performance, and that multiple-choice tests in particular tend not to measure the more complex cognitive student skills. It is possible to develop multiple-choice tests that will test higher-level skills, but it is not easy; it takes a sophisticated knowledge of test construction and usually some pretesting of items. Most faculty members do not know enough about how to do this, or they do not have the time to do it.

Milton and Edjerly (1976), analyzing teacher-designed classroom examinations, found a number of faults in the exams, one being that the questions often asked by faculty members did not represent the wide range of content in a course. For example, in a philosophy course that covered years of philosophy, five out of seven questions on the teacher-designed exam dealt with Kant. There was also a limited range of learning outcomes reflected in these exams: The emphasis was often on recall of knowledge rather than on higher-level cognitive processes. McGuire's study

(1963) of examinations given to medical students, for example, found that 50 percent of the questions analyzed tested recall and recognition of isolated information. Finally, Fredericksen (1984) found technical difficulties with teacher-made exams, such as questions that were vague, ambiguous, or unreliable or questions where the student had to figure out what the instructor was trying to elicit as an answer.

None of this information should be surprising because most college teachers really do not have any training either in teaching or in the construction of exams. This is an area that both formative and summative evaluations need to address. For example, some faculty instructional development programs have used the technique of comparing teacher examinations with their course objectives. For the most part, instructors are willing to talk about their exams and willing to take advice on how to improve their exams; this often leads the instructors to look back at objectives and to think of other teaching methods that might best accomplish them.

There should be some way of using this kind of information for summative purposes, although I am not advocating a narrow use of outcome measures. Student performance on an exam is a reflection not only of the teacher but also of what students bring to the course, including their own attitudes, motivation, and previous learning. That is one reason why it is so hard to compare examination results across instructors of the same course: Students often are not randomly distributed among course sections. At the very least, however, outcome measures can be used as a "red flag" indicator. For example, the students of an instructor who is not accomplishing his or her course objectives will not do well in the classes that build on that course. They will also not do as well as students of good teachers on comprehensive exams or on professional exams where that course material is being tested. These later outcome measures, then, become red flags that indicate potential problems in the teaching of the original course.

The Evaluation of Research and Scholarship

Something interesting has been happening recently: Institutions that were typically teaching institutions, or at least that had put little emphasis on research, suddenly are deciding, because of the glut of new teachers with doctorates, "Ah! We can easily get people who are good teachers; now let us start putting emphasis on good research as well." The president of one university said: "We are now going to enter the ranks of major research universities and expect our people to be more than good teachers; we are now going to put an emphasis on research publications."

Many institutions seem to feel that, to assess faculty members' research, all they need to do is count up the number of publications produced. What do you think the correlation is between the quantity of a faculty member's research and scholarship and its quality? I surveyed a group of department heads (Centra, 1977) in which quality was judged by use of a citation index—that is, by a count of the number of times a person was referenced by others. I found the correlation between that sort of measure of quality and the quantity of publications produced to be between 0.60 and 0.70. That is high but is hardly a perfect correlation. Why is the correlation imperfect? In addition in the studies surveyed, there were two groups that comprised about a third of each sample: the "mass producers" (those who put out a large number of papers with little or no quality) and the "perfectionists" (those who produced high-quality research but low quantity). If you are measuring productivity just by measuring numbers of publications, you are going to miss this significant group of "perfectionists."

Let us consider how, if you were the dean of a college that puts emphasis on research and scholarship, you might include a measure of quality. One possibility is to use a citation index, but the index is really not very useful for making decisions about people. It takes a year or two to get something into print, and, by the time it gets into the citation index and then cited, it may be five or six years. By that time it is often too late for use in tenure decisions. So it is a little unreasonable to use a citations index for making tenure and promotion decisions unless you are thinking of just those few faculty members who are being considered for the upper ranks within the university.

What are some other possibilities for assessing quality? Some departments give extra weight to articles that appear in the most reputable journals in the field; in this case, the departments should let teachers know which journals count the most. The other possibility is to look for continuity in research, some sort of pattern indicating that the faculty member has not just addressed a topic and then run off in another direction but that he or she is building on previous work—their own as well as others. The third possibility, and this is certainly widely used, is peer assessment. Often this involves relying on peers from outside the institution since there may not be other people within the institution who are as knowledgeable about a particular field as the professor being assessed.

The Politics of Evaluation

Piper (1983) recently conducted an interview study of department heads in institutions across the United Kingdom and found that there were certain *hidden* criteria or circumstances that department chairs used in their promotion deliberations. I will mention one or two here that appear to be interesting. One criterion concerned the consequences of the department head's decisions: If not recommending a person might mean that the position would be frozen or lost, then the department head would rather push forward the candidate. Thus, timing is critical. Another hidden criterion that is even more disturbing is that the department head would often take into account how aggressive and vindictive a faculty member might be. Somebody who is likely to become actively aggressive would get consideration whereas someone who is equally qualified but more passive would be passed over.

There are often four different factions that a college has to consider when it develops a system of faculty evaluation. The first group consists of the "purists." The purist group insists that faculty performance must be quantified and measured with microscopic precision. They want to be able to rank all 200 faculty members on campus; otherwise they feel the system is not working. Another group is called the "utopians." This group finds fault in every instrument or system devised. They want the perfect instrument, and, if they find one even partly defective, which they invariably do, they conclude that the system is worthless. The third group is called the "saboteurs." They pretend to support efforts to develop evaluation systems, but they find fault in every approach and call for endless refinements. The fourth group is referred to as the "naive." They are ready to adopt any instrument or any system without thinking through its implications or whether it will work. No doubt, on most campuses, there is a fifth group called the "realists." The realists know that whatever is put together one year may have to be modified the next. They know also that people are going to be evaluated whether you set up a system or not and that not setting up a system is worse than working on a year-to-year basis until something worthwhile evolves. This is the group to whom this chapter is addressed.

References

Aleamoni, L. M. "The Usefulness of Student Evaluations in Improving College Teaching." *Instructional Science*, 1978, *7*, 95–105.

Aleamoni, L. M., and Hexner, P. Z. "A Review of the Research on Student Evaluation and a Report on the Effect of Different Sets of Instructions on Student Course and Instructor Evaluation." *Instructional Science*, 1980, *9*, 67–84.

Braunstein, D. N., Klein, G. A., and Pachla, M. "Feedback Expectancy and Shifts in Student Ratings of College Faculty." *Journal of Applied Psychology*, 1973, *58* (2), 254–258.

Centra, J. A. "Effectiveness of Student Feedback in Modifying College Instruction." *Journal of Educational Psychology*, 1973, *65* (3), 395–401.

Centra, J. A. "Colleagues as Raters of Classroom Instruction." *Journal of Higher Education*, 1975, *46*, 327–337.

Centra, J. A. *How Universities Evaluate Faculty Performance: A Survey of Department Heads.* Research Report no. 75–56R. Princeton, N.J.: Graduate Record Examination Program, Educational Testing Service, 1977.

Cohen, P. A. "Student Ratings of Instruction and Achievement: A Meta-Analysis of Multisection Validity Studies." *Review of Educational Research*, 1981, *51* (3), 281–309.

Fredericksen, N. "The Real Test Bias: Influences of Testing on Teaching and Learning." *American Psychologist,* 1984, *39* (3), 193-202.

Grasha, A. F. *Assessing and Developing Faculty Performances: Principles and Models.* Cincinnati, Ohio: Communication and Education Associates, 1977.

Guthrie, E. R. *The Evaluation of Teaching.* Seattle: University of Washington, 1954.

McGuire, C. H. "A Process Applied to the Construction and Analysis of the Medical Examination." *Journal of Medical Education,* 1963, *38,* 556-563.

McKeachie, W. J. "Student Ratings of Faculty: A Reprise." *Academe,* 1979, *65,* 384-397.

Marsh, H. W. "Students' Evaluations of University Teaching: Dimensionality, Reliability, Validity, Potential Biases, and Utility." *Journal of Educational Psychology,* 1984, *76* (5), 707-754.

Miller, M. T. "Instructor Attitudes Toward, and Their Use of, Student Ratings of Teachers." *Journal of Educational Psychology,* 1971, *62* (3), 235-239.

Millman, J. (ed.). *Handbook of Teacher Evaluation.* Beverly Hills, Calif.: Sage, 1981.

Milton, O., and Edjerly, J. "The Testing and Grading of Students." *Change,* 1976.

Piper, D. *An Interview of Department Heads in Institutions Across the United Kingdom.* Paper presented at the Ninth International Conference on University Teaching in Dublin, Ireland, July 1983.

Remmers, H. H. "To What Extent Do Grades Influence Student Ratings of Instructors?" *Journal of Educational Research,* 1949, *21,* 314-316.

Wotruba, T. R., and Wright, P. L. "How to Develop a Teacher-Rating Instrument: A Research Approach." *Journal of Higher Education,* 1974, *46* (6), 653-663.

John A. Centra is professor and chair in higher and postsecondary education at Syracuse University and was program administrator at the Educational Testing Service from 1982 to 1986.

Instructional evaluation without professional feedback will not affect college instruction.

Instructional Evaluation as a Feedback Process

Doron H. Gil

For many years now researchers have devised and designed a variety of means to evaluate teaching in higher education for a variety of purposes (Rippey, 1981): (1) allocation of teaching or faculty resources; (2) development of awareness, sensitivity, and appreciation of teaching; (3) improvement of instruction; (4) tenure and promotion decisions; (5) program evaluation; (6) research on teaching. Yet some questions still persist: Has faculty evaluation been successful? What usually are the end products of such evaluation? Have programs been changed or instruction been improved as a result of these evaluation efforts?

The main argument of this chapter is that instructional evaluation, as it is currently conducted and practiced, has little, if any, effect on college instruction. Feedback, instead of evaluation, needs to be the main technique used in faculty development, and its primary focus should be on instructional improvement. On today's campuses, the issues of accountability, budget constraints, and public investments are generating questions about the quality and efficiency of teaching in higher education (Goldschmid, 1978), but, at the same time, new educational technology and research tools (such as videotapes and computers) are producing strategies that will allow us to enhance teaching effectiveness through feedback (Goldschmid, 1976).

L. M. Aleamoni (ed.). *Techniques for Evaluating and Improving Instruction.*
New Directions for Teaching and Learning, no. 31. San Francisco: Jossey-Bass, Fall 1987.

Feedback Versus Evaluation

Feedback, for the purposes of this chapter, is defined as information provided to instructors about their performance that includes recommendations for future improvement. As such, it is a "people process": The focus is on the instructor, not on the measurement or evaluation tools or on the product or outcomes.

The data (Aleamoni, 1978) on the improvement of instruction do not provide hard evidence that simply evaluating teaching has an effect on teaching improvement or student achievement. Facilitating conditions must also exist for improvement to occur. For example, Bergquist and Phillips (1975) argue that faculty development must deal with the attitudes of the faculty members, their philosophies and self-perceptions:

> Frequently, when introduced to methods of college instruction, a faculty member will turn away or adopt a stance of passive resistance. Central to this resistance is the attitude of the faculty member toward teaching. If he does not value teaching, or does not perceive himself as being primarily a teacher, he will not spend time learning new techniques or exploring alternative instructional methods. At the same time, he may be fearful of displaying his shortcomings as a teacher or may be resisting the values and philosophies of education that underlie many new methods or curriculum proposals. Frequently, he has neither an articulated value system concerning teaching nor a coherent philosophy of education, and the new method or proposal may inevitably find itself at odds with ill-defined values or philosophies. An effective faculty development program, then, must deal with the attitudes of the faculty member, as well as with related values, philosophies, and self-perceptions [pp. 185–186].

Many instructors carry out course evaluations only at the end of the semester. Several authors (Centra, 1972; Gage, 1974; McKeachie and Lin, 1975; and Pambookian, 1976) have provided evidence that course evaluations in midsemester can bring about changes in teaching practices. Review of this literature indicates that these evaluations were actually *feedback*, communicated to instructors in midsemester, about their teaching. Powell and O'Neal (1976) have shown that the amount of information in itself is not as crucial to a person as the amount of information that is validated via interpersonal feedback. Also, positive feedback is more desirable and has a better impact than negative feedback. For example, feedback in the form of praise and encouragement can often reduce anxiety and improve an instructor's self-concept.

Feedback and evaluation are related processes. Feedback aspires to improve faculty performance; evaluation aims to make judgments regarding its worth. Although sometimes these judgments are used to make personnel decisions, at other times these judgments are used to provide feedback to faculty regarding their performance (Whitman and Schwenk, 1982). Because feedback reduces anxiety, pinpoints strengths and weaknesses, and defines areas for improvement, it is more likely to lead to changes in performance.

Even when an evaluation includes some positive judgments about the instructor, there still appears to be no further instructional improvement. Feedback, on the other hand, has a better potential to lead to further improvement, even when it is negative.

Feedback and Instructional Improvement

There are many advantages to conducting instructional development through providing feedback. First, feedback ensures that instructors know and understand what is expected of them. Feedback starts with wherever the faculty member and his or her present instructional qualifications happen to be, rather than with where an evaluation wants this faculty member to be. This simple human element is often forgotten when one conducts instructional evaluation. Second, there is an assessment of those factors that both help and hinder better instructional performance: Does the instructor lack identifiable teaching skills? Does he or she lack an interest in the students? Is he or she aware, at all, of his or her specific teaching practices? In this way, feedback focuses on process, rather than on product; it deals with human beings, rather than with measurement tools; and it focuses on human performance, satisfaction, attitudes, and motivation.

Some claim that characteristics of good feedback are simply characteristics of good communication. One way to improve that communication is to reduce the degree of defensiveness on the part of instructors. This can be done through supportive behavior. Gibb (1951) lists the following categories of behavior as characteristic of a defensive climate: evaluation, control, neutrality, and superiority. A supportive climate, on the other hand, is characterized by the following approaches: description, problem orientation, empathy, and equality.

With feedback the consultant develops interpersonal communication with the instructor and uses support and encouragement to help him or her improve. The personal contact between the consultant and the instructor encourages reciprocal communication.

Inducing Change

People are not likely to change merely because someone tells them to. Therefore, feedback, as a mutual process that helps instructors find their own strengths and weaknesses, is an effective means of inducing change. Otherwise, when encountering negative evaluation, instructors might be inclined to rationalize: "Students don't know what's good for them"; "this isn't really important anyway"; "this observation (or instrument) isn't valid"; and so on. By becoming defensive, they foster a behavior that negates change, improvement, and growth.

Thus, evaluation, which arouses defensiveness, seldom guides the instructor to any behavioral changes. As Bergquist and Phillips (1975) put it:

> Change is a subtle and complex process. It is not encouraged by the use of an insensitive, often arbitrary, reliance on evaluative ratings of performance. Preparation for change, "unfreezing" in instructional performance, occurs when the teacher is confronted with information that is discrepant with his self-image but which does not deflate his self-esteem. This information is requested by the instructor, rather than forced on him; it is descriptive, rather than evaluative; it is concrete, rather than general; it is presented in a context of trust, rather than threat. The process of change takes place only when the instructor is presented with information, training and consultation directly related to perceived needs [p. 190].

Any change can only come from within. Evaluation of instruction and reporting the results to the instructors can only be helpful if there is an agreement, a contract between the consultant and the instructor, and if they work together. Some argue that feedback alone cannot bring about changes in behavior but that it needs to be accompanied by opportunities for practice and continued information. Aleamoni's (1978) research indicates that change is more likely to result when evaluation is coupled with consultation, but such feedback influences performance only to the extent that the individual uses the information provided.

Feedback is explanatory rather than judgmental. It is most useful when it occurs during the process of instruction and when it includes subjective comments (which evaluation often does not). It helps teachers become aware of specific and important behaviors that affect student learning; this awareness is a key to change. Feedback is a critical component in both motivating and training teachers. An interpersonal feedback process, sensitive to individual differences and carefully distinguished from evaluation procedures, can be a potent force in inducing change.

Individualized Attention and Teacher Satisfaction

So much attention has been given in recent years to individualized instruction, to education of the gifted, and to learning disabilities and reading problems that classes are no longer organized and managed as if all students were basically the same. Similarly, the educators of teachers have moved away from standardized instruction; rather, they advocate the learning of diagnostic skills that will help instructors make relevant, timely, and effective pedagogical decisions about individual learners.

University professors can be looked on as learners, each of them with individual strengths, weaknesses, capabilities, and limitations. Thus, those responsible for faculty development need to individualize faculty evaluation and development and the processes through which they reach faculty. This individualization is no easy task, taking into consideration the small number of faculty development consultants and the large number of faculty at any given college or university, as well as the likelihood of a consultant's skills and background being in evaluation and measurement rather than in human relations.

Over a decade ago, Gaff (1976) wrote: "Unless we evaluate our own programs and demonstrate that they produce results in terms of better courses or better educated students, more knowledgeable, sensitive, effective, or satisfied faculty members, or more effectively managed organizations, we will be out of business." That warning is just as pertinent today. More than a decade of retrenchments and diminished opportunities for faculty has reduced sources of stimulation and encouragement. Evaluation is often perceived as a threat. In such a climate, supportive consultants providing faculty with personal and concrete feedback on teaching that may have gone stale are important sources of stimulation.

Unfortunately, instructors who most need improvement are often those least involved with faculty development. Such instructors may wonder, "What is in it for me? Why should I go through a process of observations, workshops, and consultations?" If the threat of promotion or tenure being denied is absent, what *can* stimulate instructors to seek consultation?

James Bess (1973), in an article called "Integrating Faculty and Student Life Cycles" described this problem:

> Since prestige is derived from research reputation, the academic social system and, in some cases, misguided personal propensities would seem to be leading faculty to perform tasks which may not satisfy their most basic needs. Many are drawn, in other words, to continue to do research in the belief that its career rewards will provide higher personal satisfactions. In a way, then, they are thus seduced into giving relatively less attention through teaching to meeting student needs—an activity which might, under different conditions, yield them profound satisfactions in great abundance.
>
> Students at most institutions under present circumstances are also not able to fulfill their most important needs,

particularly those which involve their developing person-
alities. Colleges and universities usually give greater attention to establish structures designed to help students acquire
cognitive knowledge, in service of broad liberal education
and/or, presumably, career preparation. Satisfaction of student needs for emotional and interpersonal growth and for
self-knowledge are, at best, by-products of the college experience. They are rarely explicit goals of the institution. Hence,
at least two of the three main constituencies on our college
and university campuses (faculty and students) may exist
under conditions antithetical, or at least not conducive, to
meeting the most profound of their collective and individual
needs [p. 377].

The need to teach well and to gain the satisfactions that go with it
are chronic as well as current faculty needs, even if, for some, these needs
seem to go unrecognized. Faculty development consultants are in a position to convince faculty that a shared attention to teaching with an emphasis on informed and useful feedback has a fair chance of raising any
teacher's level of satisfaction.

Thus, feedback can help instructors focus on their own teaching
style (rather than on teaching products) and on students as human beings
(rather than on course content). It can also help increase instructors' enjoy-
ment of teaching (and diminish any sense of being bored with it). Feedback can help teachers not only improve their teaching practices but also
change their attitudes toward the act (or art) of teaching, so that they
perceive it as a challenging activity.

Faculty Self-Awareness and Faculty Education Relations

Most people do not see themselves as others see them. Blackburn
and Clark (1975) reported little agreement between faculty self-ratings of
overall teaching effectiveness and ratings by students, colleagues, or administrators. The last three groups did agree substantially in their ratings of
the teachers.

Centra (1973) studied teachers from five colleges and compared
teachers' self-ratings with student ratings. Not only was there lack of agreement between self-ratings and student ratings but there was also the tendency on the part of the teachers to give themselves better ratings than
their students assigned them. These differences provide a starting point
for a consultant in the process of feedback and education, for faculty need
to be taught about teaching, about themselves, about the ways students
learn, and about what prevents students from learning.

Feedback, as part of an instructional improvement and evaluation program, can stimulate faculty to undertake this learning and can motivate them to continue with workshops and further consultations. Many faculty, from a variety of fields, have had little exposure to the great body of scholarship about teaching and learning. Many who experience difficulties with teaching are inhibited in seeking help or even in sharing their problems with colleagues. Few enroll in workshops on teaching; even instructors who receive poor student ratings often do not do anything about their teaching.

If, on the other hand, offices of instructional development will assume some responsiblity for the personal as well as the professional growth of the faculty, it will, in the long run, have a positive effect on students as well.

Conclusions and Recommendations

McKeachie, Lin, Moffett, and Daugherty (1978) found that instructors classified as "facilitator-person" were more effective than other teachers (those occupying roles of "expert" and "authority") in terms of student motivation for taking additional psychology courses. They hypothesized that these teachers will be more effective with respect to measures of student thinking, attitudes, and motivation. They concluded that the effect of the teacher as a model is enhanced if the teacher is seen as a person, rather than as someone who only teaches content.

With the many problems existing in today's society—child abuse and neglect, broken families, violence, rape, and drugs—young adults do not have a sufficient number of positive role models to follow. If those involved with instructional development can help provide them with more faculty who serve as role models, it could be a service both to the students' needs and to society's as well.

Faculty consultants, whose time has been heavily engaged in evaluating instruction, need to devote more time to helping both faculty and students through effective feedback techniques and the development of communication and interpersonal skills.

To promote feedback, offices of instructional development and colleges of education need to generate creative ideas. A feedback system should not replace evaluation systems but should be complementary to evaluation. Faculty development consultants need to possess more process skills, such as counseling and communication, and be sensitive and self-aware individuals who can work cooperatively with university instructors. This may call for reorganization of instructional development offices and of departments of education, with an emphasis on the lifelong education of university instructors.

64

References

Aleamoni, L. M. "The Usefulness of Student Evaluations in Improving College Teaching." *Instructional Science,* 1978, *7,* 95–105.

Bergquist, W. H., and Phillips, S. R. "Components of an Effective Faculty Development Program." *Journal of Higher Education,* 1975, *46,* 177–211.

Bess, J. L. "Integrating Faculty and Student Life Cycles." *Review of Educational Research,* 1973, *43,* 377–403.

Blackburn, R. T., and Clark, M. J. "An Assessment of Faculty Performance: Some Correlates Between Administrator, Colleague, Student, and Self-Ratings." *Sociology of Education,* 1975, *48,* 242–256.

Centra, J. A. *Strategies for Improving College Teaching.* Vol. 8. Washington, D.C.: Educational Resources Information Center (ERIC), 1973. (ED 071 616)

Centra, J. A. "Self-Ratings of College Teachers: A Comparison with Student Ratings." *Journal of Educational Measurement,* 1973, *10,* 287–295.

Gaff, J. G. "Faculty Development: The State of the Art." In D. W. Vermilye (ed.), *Individualizing the System: Current Issues in Higher Education.* San Francisco: Jossey-Bass, 1976.

Gage, N. L. "Students' Ratings of College Teaching: Their Justification and Proper Use." In N. S. Clasman, and B. R. Killait (eds.), *Second UCSB Conference on Effective Teaching.* Santa Barbara: University of California, 1974.

Gibb, J. R. "The Effects of Group Size and Threat Reduction Upon Creativity in a Problem-Solving Situation." *American Psychologist,* 1951, *6,* 324–330.

Goldschmid, M. L. "Teaching and Learning in Higher Education: Recent Trends." *Higher Education,* 1976, *5,* 437–456.

Goldschmid, M. L. "The Evaluation and Improvement of Teaching in Higher Education." *Higher Education,* 1978, *7,* 221–245.

McKeachie, W. J., and Lin, Y-G. *Use of Student Ratings in Evaluation of College Teaching.* Ann Arbor, Mich.: National Institute of Education, 1975.

McKeachie, W. J., Lin, Y-G., Moffett, M., and Daugherty, M. "Effective Teaching: Facilitative Versus Directive Style." *Teaching of Psychology,* 1978, *5,* 193–194.

Pambookian, H. S. "Discrepancy Between Instructor and Student Evaluation of Instruction: Effect on Instructor." *Instructional Science,* 1976, *5,* 63–75.

Powell, R. S., and O'Neal, E. C. "Communication Feedback and Duration as Determinants of Accuracy, Confidence, and Differentiation in Interpersonal Perception." *Journal of Personality and Social Psychology,* 1976, *34,* 746–756.

Rippey, R. M. *The Evaluation of Teaching in Medical Schools.* New York: Springer, 1981.

Whitman, N., and Schwenk, T. "Faculty Evaluation as a Means of Faculty Development." *Journal of Family Practice,* 1982, *14,* 1097–1101.

Doron H. Gil is a research associate in the Office of Medical Education in the College of Medicine at the University of Arizona.

A successful comprehensive faculty evaluation program may
serve as a model for community and junior colleges.

A Faculty Evaluation
Model for Community
and Junior Colleges

Raoul A. Arreola

In many institutions of higher education today there is a pressing need to establish some form of faculty evaluation system. In many cases, the primary impetus for an institution entering the arena of faculty evaluation is a mandate from the state legislature, the board of regents, the institution's president, or a similar controlling authority. Whatever the source, a directive is issued, a committee appointed, and a group of faculty or administrators or both finds itself in the position of having to design and implement a faculty evaluation program. Faculty members generally meet the introduction of faculty evaluation programs with something less than enthusiasm; in fact, they are often overtly hostile to the idea. The key to overcoming this resistance on the part of the faculty is to (1) involve the faculty in the design of the program, (2) design a comprehensive system containing more than a student-rating component, and (3) make sure that the system recognizes and fairly values a variety of faculty assignments and competences.

I have worked with many community and junior colleges around the country on faculty evaluation and faculty development. In contrast to four-year colleges and universities, the community and junior colleges

L. M. Aleamoni (ed.). *Techniques for Evaluating and Improving Instruction.*
New Directions for Teaching and Learning, no. 31. San Francisco: Jossey-Bass, Fall 1987.

seem much better able to focus on the evaluation of teaching and to incorporate it into their overall decision making—in particular, into their promotion and tenure stuctures. Apparently that is because teaching, at community and junior colleges, is considered an important mission in and of itself.

Many of these colleges must try to incorporate faculty evaluation and faculty development within faculties that are unionized. I have found, however, that unionized faculty—and the institutions that have unionized faculty—surprisingly enough are very responsive to faculty evaluation. Other observers have also reported that the linkage of faculty evaluation with faculty development is more readily accepted in a unionized situation, perhaps because clearly defined agreements about many aspects of faculty employment have already been reached at the bargaining table.

This chapter describes an approach that has proved successful at ten out of twelve community and junior colleges. (The lack of success in two colleges can be traced to a change in administration; the new administrators did not pursue the program.) This strategy for developing a comprehensive faculty evaluation program integrates or links all aspects of faculty performance, rather than focusing simply on teaching. Using this approach, the colleges were able to develop the specifics of their own systems, rather than having a consultant tell them how to evaluate their faculty.

Determining and Weighting Faculty Roles

The first step with these colleges was to ask them to determine the faculty role model of the institution. In other words, the faculty needed to decide what ought to be evaluated. Most institutions assume that teaching is to be evaluated, but they have not always given careful attention to what teaching includes and to the other responsibilities, such as advising, community service, and research, that faculty members are expected to carry out. The faculty should examine the various possible roles that they play by generating a listing of them and then determining which of them ought to be evaluated. Obviously, there will be different combinations for different institutions depending on the makeup of the institution.

Once the decision has been made as to what roles the faculty play and what ought to be evaluated, the second step is to determine how much value or weight should be placed on each role. For example, suppose that teaching, faculty service, and community service are the roles that are to be evaluated. One then needs to establish the optimal values, or weights of these roles: For example, teaching activities might be weighted at no less than 50 percent and no more than 85 percent of the overall evaluation, faculty service at no less than 10 percent and no more than 30 percent, and so on. The weighting process communicates to the faculty at a particular institution that a faculty member cannot say, "All I want to do is teach, and I want my entire evaluation based solely on my teaching." Nor can she or he say, "I want faculty service to count for 50 percent of my evaluation."

In junior and community colleges, the faculty role model is likely to include teaching and activities closely related to it (such as advising), as well as various faculty and community services. Because of the congruence among expected roles at these colleges, the weighting process may be easier than at universities, where a greater diversity of roles and the relative importance of research and teaching create chronic problems.

Specifying and weighting faculty roles provides an indication of the value structure of the institution, and faculty members should play a major part in determining both.

Defining Roles and Gaining Information

The third step is to define each of the roles in terms of readily observable or documentable achievements, products, and performances. For example, how is teaching defined so that it can be evaluated? Teaching can be defined as being composed of instructional delivery skills, knowledge of subject, enthusiasm, and concern for students. Teaching can also be defined to include a wide range of instructional design skills, such as test construction, development of syllabi, course organization, and so forth. Various measures of the content expertise of the instructor could be added, as well as dimensions of record keeping and management. The same definition process must be followed for the other roles that are going to be evaluated.

The fourth step is to determine which source, or sources, should provide the information on which the evaluation is to be based. If one is going to assess instructional delivery skills, for example, where should the information come from? Students? Yes because they observe the teacher's delivery during every class period. Peers? No, unless one institutes a peer visitation policy. Self? Probably. Department chair? Probably not, unless the chair engages in systematic visits. One must go through this process for each and every role that is defined.

The fifth step is to determine how much value or weight should be placed on the information provided by the various sources selected for each role. If one is going to have a department chair evaluation component, for example, how much weight is to be placed on that particular source of information? These weightings, too, are likely to reflect a particular institution's values: Some institutions place great value on what students say, but other institutions weigh peer evaluation heavily. Any evaluation system that is going to be put into place has to have a clearly defined set of values. A good evaluation system would be one in which congruence between what was observed and what was valued resulted in a positive evaluation.

Arriving at a Matrix

Figure 1 puts into a matrix form the end result of the process just described. Such a matrix could form the basis of an effective evaluation system for many junior and community colleges. The most difficult step in arriving at such a matrix is gaining consensus about roles, weighting, and sources of information. In colleges with a high degree of faculty autonomy, a survey of faculty opinions, followed by discussion, agreement among faculty, and acceptance by the administration, is a probable course. In other institutions, faculty may have to struggle with administrators to get their collective views recognized and accepted.

The matrix in Figure 1 does not go beyond a general level of specification. Obviously, there are diverse ways of gaining input from specified sources. Equally important, one matrix may not fit all faculty, even within a small community or junior college. The wide range of faculty roles, departmental functions, and disciplines makes it difficult to arrive at a simple matrix suitable to a large university.

A Model for Community and Junior Colleges

Assuming all of the above has been done, how does one implement an evaluation system like this? This section describes how this was done in a number of community and junior colleges involved in the Southern Regional Education Board (SREB) project of 1975-76.

The procedure followed in implementing evaluation systems with the SREB colleges was first to assume that all of the information from the various sources can be summarized on a common scale (for example, a scale of 1 to 5). It is a simple matter to design student-rating forms that report student input on such a scale, and ratings from many students can be combined relatively easily or averaged to provide an overall rating for a particular course. Peer ratings, however, in which small a group of peers are reviewing course materials, tests, syllabi, and so on, may at first appear to be more difficult to report on a common 1-to-5 scale. However, a peer review committee could take the simple approach of having each committee member subjectively review all the materials and assign an overall rating from 1 to 5. The committee could then report an average, or they could simply vote on a particular overall rating and report that. Alternately, a peer review committee could take a much more detailed and objective approach, in which specific criteria and checklists are developed adapted to a 1 to 5 scale, and used to evaluate the various instructional materials reviewed. The point is that it is a relatively easy procedure to

Figure 1. Example of Data-Gathering Specification Matrix

Role

Sources

TEACHING	STUDENTS	PEERS	SELF	DEPT. CHAIR
1) Instructional Delivery Skills	Questionnaire		Self Report or Questionnaire	
2) Instructional Design Skills	Questionnaire	Peer Review of Materials	Self Report	
3) Content Expertise		Peer Analysis of Course Content	Self Report	Interview
4) Record Keeping/Management			Self Report	Checklist Grade Distributions

design any form, procedure, or protocol that generates summary information on a common scale.

Now, let us assume the ratings that we obtained from the various sources for a particular instructor are as follows: The students assigned a 4 looking at instructional delivery and instructional design; the peers assigned a 5 looking at design skill and content expertise; self, 4; and department chair, 3. Remember, the area of concentration is still only teaching, so the same thing will have to be done for other agreed-upon roles. Assume the weighting factors were: (1) student input to count 75 percent; (2) peer input to count 15 percent; (3) self, 5 percent, and (4) department chair, 5 percent. Now we take the composite ratings from these sources and multiply them by the weights that reflect how much their input is valued. By summing these multiplied values, we a get a composite role rating of 4.10 for this particular example. That rating does not come from any one individual or any one administrator; it is a mosaic pieced together to reflect the input from all these various sources on an instructor's teaching. To use this information, we must recognize that different faculty may have different assignments; not every faculty member is going to have precisely the same teaching load or precisely the same research load, although at community and junior colleges there is more similarity than at four-year colleges or universities.

Take a hypothetical Professor Jones who has negotiated an agreement with his department chair. The department chair has given him the teaching assignment for the year, and Professor Jones indicates the type of research and community service he plans to do. They examine the goals and objectives that Professor Jones has set for himself and that the department chair has agreed will carry out the necessary roles of the department. They then generate a distribution of weighting factors that fairly accurately represents the assignment of Professor Jones. If Professor Jones's teaching is weighted at 50 percent, however, that does not mean that he has a 50 percent teaching load—only that, when it is time to evaluate Professor Jones, his composite teaching rating is going to count for 50 percent of his overall evaluation. Similarly, Professor Jones's evaluation of research is weighted at 35 percent of his overall evaluation, faculty service at 10 percent, and community service, 5 percent.

In a unionized situation, such negotiations take place at the beginning of the school year. Assume that Professor Jones has taken the minimum weighting for teaching, the maximum weighting for research, and the minimum weighting for faculty service and community service. These weights reflect his assignment for the year and represent the emphasis he will place on these activities during the year. When each of these roles is evaluated at the end of the year, Professor Jones is given a composite rating from the agreed-on and weighted sources. These can now be combined with Professor Jones's designated roles, as shown in Figure 2. The

Figure 2. Computation of Professor Jones's Overall Composite Rating

ROLE	ASSIGNED WEIGHT	X	COMPOSITE ROLE RATING	=	WEIGHTED COMPOSITE RATING
TEACHING	50%	X	3.50	=	1.75
RESEARCH	35%	X	4.20	=	1.47
FACULTY SERVICE	10%	X	3.60	=	.36
COMMUNITY SERVICE	5%	X	3.60	=	.18
OVERALL COMPOSITE RATING				=	3.76

separate figures in the right-hand column reflect both emphasis and quality of service. The overall composite rating, 3.76, can be thought of as an index of success.

Let us take another hypothetical faculty member, Professor Smith. She has a different assignment; she is not doing any research at all, but she attaches the same weight to faculty and community service as does Professor Jones. Teaching is weighted at 85 percent. Her overall composite rating is 3.77, as presented in Figure 3. This reflects a different kind of assignment for a different faculty member as well as different levels of performance.

In sum, however, these two professors are being evaluated as performing at the same level in doing what they agreed to do for the institution. They may not be doing the same things, because no two faculty ever do, but one cannot say, "Well, this professor did more, so he received a better evaluation." Instead, one can say, "Professor Jones agreed to do these things in these proportions and has been judged as being successful to the degree indicated for each. Professor Smith has agreed to do those things in those proportions and has been judged to be similarly successful." The composite gives, then, a real basis for comparison, rather than trying to compare apples with oranges. Let us see how this evaluation system can be applied to some practical decision making.

Applications to Decisions on Promotion, Tenure, and Merit Pay

If a college had a system of this sort in place, promotions could be based in part on the achievement of a specified minimum overall composite rating for a certain number of years. For example, a policy could be established that says a minimum overall composite rating of 3.4 or 3.5 for the last three consecutive years will be required for promotion from assistant professor to associate professor. The question of how one establishes that number is another issue, for it requires faculty and administration agreement as to the minimum level of excellence required for retention as well as for promotion at various levels.

Similarly, one could make tenure decisions based in part on the achievement of a specified average overall composite rating for the entire length of time that the faculty member has worked for the institution. For example, one could specify that an average overall composite rating must be maintained over a specified number of years before tenure will be awarded. If the average composite ratings are used over a span of time, then an instructor could have a bad year and a good year but might still be able to maintain a specified level of performance (say, an average overall composite rating of 3.2) for seven years and thus be eligible for tenure.

Finally, merit pay raises could also be determined as a direct func-

Figure 3. Computation of Professor Smith's Overall Composite Rating

ROLE	ASSIGNED WEIGHT	X	COMPOSITE ROLE RATING	=	WEIGHTED COMPOSITE RATING
TEACHING	85%	X	3.85	=	3.27
FACULTY SERVICE	10%	X	3.50	=	.35
COMMUNITY SERVICE	5%	X	3.00	=	.15
OVERALL COMPOSITE RATING				=	3.77

tion of these overall composite ratings. For example, one could first determine a merit unit for the department by taking the total amount of money that is available for raises and dividing it by the grand total of all the ratings of the faculty in that department. (Of course, this process could work for a division or even a whole college, rather than just a department). Say that a department has $10,000 for its merit raises. The overall composite ratings of its seven faculty members add up to a total of 26.92. Dividing that into the $10,000 results in $371.50 becoming the merit unit amount for that department. The determination of individual raises, then, is the simple matter of multiplying the merit unit by an individual's composite ratings. Professor Johnson with a 2.76 overall composite would receive a raise of $1,025. Professor Stevens with a 4.35 rating would receive $1,616. It might be that a department would set a minimum composite ratings figure (2.0, for example) that would establish whether a faculty member were eligible for any merit raise at all. No one below that figure would receive a raise, and their rating scores would not be used in arriving at the merit unit.

Conclusion

Many faculty members have a fear of numbers. Opposition to student ratings has often centered on the significance of supposed differences in performance of tenths or hundredths of a point. Is 3.53 significantly different from 3.57? But numbers as the foregoing examples show, make it possible to arrive at a basis for comparison at least as accurate as "pretty good," as compared with "all right" or "OK" or "doing a good job." More important, whatever system is used to account for differences in faculty roles as well as in quality of performance, it must be administered with a keen respect for the human services being performed and the human beings performing them.

Reference

Arreola, R. A. "A Strategy for Developing a Comprehensive Faculty Evaluation System." *Engineering Education*, December 1979, 70 (3), 239-244.

Raoul A. Arreola is professor and chair of the Department of Education at the Center for the Health Sciences, the University of Tennessee, Memphis.

Practical advice is offered about setting up comprehensive
systems of instructional improvement and evaluation.

Some Practical Approaches
for Faculty and Administrators

Lawrence M. Aleamoni

As the authors in this sourcebook have shown, the last decade and a half
has seen much research into the particulars of evaluating faculty, and a
large portion of this research has been concerned with student ratings.
During the same period, student ratings have become the primary source
of information in colleges and universities; some institutions depend
heavily on them in reaching decisions about faculty performance as
teachers. This accumulated research and practice have an important bear-
ing for virtually every institution on the practical problems of setting up a
comprehensive system of instructional evaluation.

The Faculty Member's Viewpoint

From the perspective of a faculty member, what should be done
about instructional development? The faculty member's first concern is
whether evaluation information can be useful in a formative sense; in
other words, can the faculty member use that information to improve his
or her performance, can he or she set up some time frame for improvement, and so on? This means that the evaluation system must cover
enough areas so that its results can say to the faculty member who is being
evaluated, "Here are the areas of strengths and weaknesses, and here in the

L. M. Aleamoni (ed.). *Techniques for Evaluating and Improving Instruction.*
New Directions for Teaching and Learning, no. 31. San Francisco: Jossey-Bass, Fall 1987.

areas of weakness are some things that you ought to do, and here are some resources you may be able to use to get some help."

In order to measure and evaluate instructional effectiveness accurately, one needs to set up criteria and guidelines for that evaluation. This first step is accomplished most effectively at the departmental level. With the encouragement and input of the departmental faculty, one should be able to come up with a list of approximately twenty-five or more criteria that the faculty can agree on; then the departmental faculty should develop guidelines to use in evaluating those criteria. Those guidelines and criteria become the basis for peer evaluation within the department. Ideally, peer evaluation is conducted by three-person peer review committees that are set up for each faculty member.

In working with departments over the years, I have found that, while faculty members want criteria for effective instruction that they can agree on, they are reluctant to give the time necessary to develop guidelines to evaluate those criteria. How does one set up the guidelines to evaluate those criteria? One of the ways, of course, is to gather from all departmental faculty members samples of the materials they would provide for each of the specified criteria and then try to set up some guidelines for evaluating levels of adequacy, importance, and so on.

Thus, one of the first steps in setting up a comprehensive system is to agree on the use of multiple components, then define the criteria needed for each component, and then begin setting up the guidelines that faculty will use in conducting the evaluation. In discussions with promotion and tenure committees from the departmental all the way up to the university level, I have noticed that upper-level committees and administrators usually model their evaluation criteria and guidelines on those of the departments. This means that, if the job is done well at the departmental level, then it will be done well all the way up the line. On the other hand, if the department has not established clear criteria and guidelines, then the other committees will begin imposing their own standards. It is imperative that departmental faculty be aware that, if they do not develop their own standards, someone else will impose his or her own.

The Administrative Viewpoint

Now, looking at an evaluation system from an administrative point of view, one can see clearly that, if one wants faculty to take seriously any comprehensive instructional evaluation system that both serves improvement purposes and is used for personnel decisions, then faculty will have to be convinced of the administration's commitment to the system. This commitment must be stated clearly and followed up by the provision of the resources and support necessary to get the system established.

In 1982, the University of Arizona faculty senate passed a series of sixteen recommendations on how instruction ought to be weighed in comparison to research. The original study that gave rise to the recommendations had been delayed for two years because the deans had questioned the sampling used. The faculty senate committee reran the study and finally had the recommendations passed in January of 1982. These recommendations are now finally being implemented. What this example points out is that, if teaching is to be a primary function on a campus and if the faculty are to believe in the college's commitment to teaching then the administration must take care of a number of important tasks, such as: (1) formally endorsing the importance of instruction in the reward system, (2) seeing that an evaluation system functions fairly and well, (3) the support necessary to train teaching assistants and new faculty. If the administration can show the faculty that it is willing to provide support, then the program will work.

Another thing that administrators need to do is to involve the faculty in the decision making. The faculty must feel involved in the process leading to agreement on the criteria and guidelines for evaluation, since these can directly affect faculty members' lives.

Questions About Comprehensive Evaluation Systems

Numerous questions arise as a comprehensive evaluation system is established and once it is in place. For example, what of those systems that have come about by a reverse process—that is, evaluations that have come about primarily because of the need to make personnel decisions? And should the committees, procedures, and activities necessary to such evaluation be separated from those dealing with teaching development?

If there is any simple answer to both questions, it is that there should be close interaction between an administration and faculty. Faculty and administrators play legitimate roles in both personnel decisions and faculty development. Making clear what these roles are and operating from a consensus in both matters are desirable goals. Obviously, many parts of an evaluation system—such as the diagnostic parts of ascertaining just how well a faculty member does what he or she is committed to do—are also useful to faculty development. But that does not mean that the basic structures for evaluation, the means by which faculty achieve tenure, promotion, and salary increases, need to be or should be the same as for faculty development. Evaluation, as various chapters of this sourcebook have pointed out, carries some threat; development occurs best within a nonthreatening, supportive climate.

A further implication is that faculty development may be most effective when the improvements it is trying to bring about are, in fact, acknowledged within the reward system; in other words, the values and results of evaluations for personnel purposes should be congruent with the kind of performance that faculty development is trying to encourage. To this end, some administrations and faculty have brought activities related to instructional improvement into the reward system and accorded them the same weight as activities demonstrating research productivity.

A closely related question is how does a faculty member or department offset the inevitable tendency for productivity of a visible kind—published research or creative work—to count more than teaching as judgments are made at a higher level? There are no simple answers here. Institutional visibility, like winning football teams, count for a great deal at the higher levels. A good teacher with a poor publication record may well get a strong recommendation from the department, but, at the college and university levels, that individual is likely to receive fewer rewards than someone with a strong publication record. In part, this is because the evidence set forth about teaching is often not convincing: Review committees can easily be provided with offprints, and letters from outside scholars can support an individual's research; seldom is any such testimony forthcoming about teaching. This situation argues for more careful attention at the departmental level to producing evidence of excellence in teaching. Indeed, an increasing sophistication in evaluating teaching can improve the quality of evidence related to performance. Departments can also gather much more information about teaching (such as course syllabi, tests, assignments, and innovations methodology) than they commonly do. Peers can examine and evaluate such material much as they now evaluate research. If these practices were to become routine, faculty members might well expand their vision of teaching and have clearer answers to that age-old question, "What is good teaching, anyhow?"

In conclusion, there is no escaping the fact that evaluating teaching and fostering good teaching are closely related activities. At best, they can function as complementary activities, but, even at worst, they should not be seen as adversarial enterprises.

Lawrence M. Aleamoni is professor of educational psychology and director of the Office of Instructional Research and Development at the University of Arizona.

*Unifying elements of the preceding chapters point the way to
stronger efforts for the evaluation and development
of faculty as teachers.*

Concluding Comments

Lawrence M. Aleamoni

These chapters represent the most current thinking by nationally recognized experts on the issues and developments in the field of instructional development and evaluation. Even though all issues and developments are not covered by these chapters, ample information is provided to guide faculty and administrators in practical applications.

Common Themes

Several unifying threads run through the preceding chapters. First, a comprehensive system of instructional evaluation needs to be established with various components differentially weighted at the departmental level. The primary goals of such a system would be feedback for improvement purposes and then use of information for personnel decision making.

Second, student ratings or evaluations should be one of the components of a comprehensive system but should not be expected to carry 100 percent (or even 80 percent) of the weight.

Third, experienced instructional development consultants should be used to provide evaluative feedback to the teaching faculty and to guide them in their use of that feedback in their instructional improvement efforts.

Fourth, university and college administrations must make a stated commitment to instruction and formally place it in the promotion-tenure reward system if it is to be taken seriously by faculty.

L. M. Aleamoni (ed.). *Techniques for Evaluating and Improving Instruction.*
New Directions for Teaching and Learning, no. 31. San Francisco: Jossey-Bass, Fall 1987.

Fifth, student governments have a role to play in the instructional development and evaluation process. This role should be coordinated with the professionals responsible for that process at each institution.

Recent History and Future Directions

As student ratings have become widely accepted, faculty development efforts have also been strengthened in a majority of colleges and universities. Formal research on evaluating teaching spans at least sixty years, though the great increase in such research is a phenomenon of the last twenty years, and, during the most recent period, faculty development has been taken up in practical ways in hundreds of colleges and universities. It, too, has generated a literature, though formal, controlled research, perhaps because of the difficulty of conducting it, is not as much in evidence as are studies of evaluating teaching. Clearly the literature points out that teaching can be evaluated and provides many examples of ways of going about it. Though there is not as clearly defined a supporting theory underlying faculty development, there is an abundance of descriptive data on how individual colleges and universities have engaged in effective and varied faculty development programs.

In both areas, general practices lag after theory and models. Student evaluation is one case in point: The particulars of how to do it well and of what it may yield are well established, but how student evaluations are actually carried out on many campuses and the uses to which they are put leave much to be desired. The same could be said of incorporating student ratings into the more comprehensive evaluation systems by which personnel decisions are made. Clearly, we now evaluate faculty performance more than we did before, and, fairly clearly, we now have better means to do it than are commonly employed. Whether better evaluation has actually become the norm over the past ten or twenty years is harder to argue.

Faculty development is closely related to faculty evaluation. The parallel development of the two may rest on no more complex explanation than the fact that an increased emphasis on evaluating faculty naturally has provoked the question, "What is to be done with or follow from what the evaluations have revealed?" While the administrators have insisted that the faculty should be more strenuously evaluated, the faculty have insisted that they should be given correspondingly greater support.

In the past twenty years, teaching has gained a greater share of evaluators' attention, perhaps because students were both numerous and obstreperous in the late sixties. The general charge was abroad that faculties were neglecting undergraduate teaching in favor of research. Today, faculty development is still closely associated with the development of teaching capacities, just as the evaluation of faculty services still emphasizes the evaluation of teaching. As many of the preceding chapters point out, few faculty would choose or are allowed to single out teaching as their sole activity; thus, there is a need to develop faculty in relation to all of the roles they are asked to fill. Evaluating teaching is but one necessary component in evaluating and developing faculty competence, and, while the focus in this volume has been primarily on teaching, we have not meant to minimize the importance of the whole range of competences that must be fostered.

The recent attention focused on improving undergraduate education emphasizes the importance of improving our efforts in both evaluating and developing faculty as teachers. Various reports resulting from the Carnegie Commission Report (National Governors' Association, 1986) have also called attention to the wider responsibilities of faculty for curriculum, governance, and scholarship. Comprehensive faculty development programs not only aim at improving individual competences in teaching but also have the larger aim of enhancing the quality of education. We hope that administrators, faculty, members of governing boards, legislators, students, faculty development specialists, and others can use the information presented in these chapters to develop successful instructional improvement programs.

Reference

National Governors' Association. *Time for Results: The Governors' 1981 Report on Education*. Washington, D.C.: National Governors' Association, 1986.

Lawrence M. Aleamoni is professor of educational psychology and director of the Office of Instructional Research and Development at the University of Arizona.

Further references on instructional improvement and evaluation are described.

Additional Sources and Information

Joseph J. Stevens

The number of publications on instructional evaluation and improvement has grown substantially in the last decade. It is virtually impossible to produce a short bibliography that is both intensive and extensive. The following bibliography was therefore generated with certain restrictions: First, only recent materials were reviewed—essentially, those published during the last five years (although some earlier materials were also included). Second, resources were included only if their primary focus was on instructional evaluation, effectiveness, or improvement at the postsecondary level. Third, in the references on instructional evaluation, there was a strong bias toward evaluation by students; this bias, however, is not only that of the current bibliography but, unfortunately, also one of current institutional practice. And, finally, this bibliography was compiled with an explicit bias toward the inclusion of articles that applied methodological techniques that are relatively uncommon or novel in the instructional literature.

Abrami, P. C. "Dimensions of Effective College Instruction." *Review of Higher Education*, 1985, *8*, 221-228.
     This article provides a good critical review of a decade of research into the dimensions or factors that characterize effective college instructors.

L. M. Aleamoni (ed.). *Techniques for Evaluating and Improving Instruction.*
New Directions for Teaching and Learning, no. 31. San Francisco: Jossey-Bass, Fall 1987.

The author suggests the use of alternative methods in this area and advises caution in the use of such dimensions for decision making.

Abrami, P. C., Leventhal, L., and Perry, R. P. "Educational Seduction." *Review of Educational Research*, 1982, *52*, 446–464.
This review of research on the "Dr. Fox" effect (the influence of instructor personality on student ratings) includes a meta-analysis of findings. Suggestions are made for improvement of the paradigm and a change in the interpretative focus of such studies.

Abrami, P. C., and Mizener, D. A. "Student/Instructor Attitude Similarity, Student Ratings, and Course Performance." *Journal of Educational Psychology*, 1985, *77*, 693–702.
Using two different attitude scales in two studies, this article reports modest relationships between student ratings and perceived attitude similarity, and between similarity and course grades. These relations decreased when instructor effects were removed. The findings fail to support a bias interpretation.

Abrami, P. C., Perry, R. P., and Leventhal, L. "The Relationship Between Student Personality Characteristics, Teacher Ratings, and Student Achievement." *Journal of Educational Psychology*, 1982, *74*, 111–125.
This study found no consistent relationship between student ratings of effectiveness and student personality characteristics. Relationships were found between ratings and perceived personality characteristics of the instructor.

Aleamoni, L. M. "Developing a Comprehensive System to Improve and Reward Instructional Effectiveness." *Resources in Education*, 1984, *19*, (1). (ED 245 765)
The author suggests the integration of instructional evaluation and improvement methodology within a framework of administrative involvement and institutional reward and support.

Banz, M. L., and Rodgers, J. L. "Dimensions Underlying Student Ratings of Instruction: A Multidimensional Scaling Analysis." *American Educational Research Journal*, 1985, *22*, 267–272.
Using a methodology uncommon in the area, this article concludes that instructor intensity, course structure, and departmental affiliation are the most salient dimensions underlying student ratings. Other commonly assessed dimensions (such as enthusiasm and student relations) showed either negligible or moderate relationships.

Basow, S. A., and Distenfeld, M. S. "Teacher Expressiveness: More Important for Male Teachers Than Female Teachers?" *Journal of Educational Psychology*, 1985, *77*, 45–52.

The possibility of an interaction between teacher expressiveness and the sex of the instructor is explored. The authors underscore the need for consideration of sex of the instructor as a variable in studies examining teacher performance and teacher characteristics.

Braskamp, L. A., Brandenburg, D. C., and Ory, J. C. *Evaluating Teaching Effectiveness: A Practical Guide.* Beverly Hills: Sage, 1984.

This is an excellent guidebook for the user of evaluation materials and methods. It is not a guide for teaching improvement, but it covers well the major issues in the development or application of an instructional evaluation system. It also provides systematic references to related literature.

Cadwell, J., and Jenkins, J. "Effects of the Semantic Similarity of Items on Student Ratings of Instructors." *Journal of Educational Psychology,* 1985, 77, 383–393.

This article suggests that the robust structure of factor analyses of student-rating forms may be in part due to the semantic similarity of items rather than a function of underlying facets or traits of instructor behavior. The strength of this conclusion is limited by an analogue procedure and a failure to consider the impact of semantic similarity on construct validity.

Centra, J. A. *Determining Faculty Effectiveness: Assessing Teaching, Research, and Service for Personnel Decisions and Improvements.* San Francisco: Jossey-Bass, 1979.

This is a research-based guide to the assessment and evaluation of faculty. It reviews self, student, and peer evaluations in the light of research results and considers the legal implications and decision-making processes related to faculty evaluation.

Centra, J. A. "Research Productivity and Teaching Effectiveness." *Research in Higher Education,* 1983, *18,* 379–389.

This study found that the relationship between research productivity and teaching effectiveness was either nonexistent or so modest that it is unlikely that one affects the other.

Cohen, P. A. "Effectiveness of Student-Rating Feedback for Improving College Instruction: A Meta-Analysis of Findings." *Research in Higher Education,* 1980, *13,* 321–341.

The author reviews the effectiveness of student-ratings feedback and concludes that modest gains in instructional improvement occur that are augmented when consultation accompanies feedback. The conclusion is limited by the fact that only twenty-two studies are considered.

Cohen, P. A. "Student Ratings of Instruction and Student Achievement: A Meta-Analysis of Multisection Validity Studies." *Review of Educational Research,* 1981, *51,* 281–309.

This article reviews forty-one independent validity studies that relate student ratings to student achievement. It provides support for a moderate effect size that may vary depending on the dimension of effectiveness that is related to achievement. The author concludes that student ratings are a valid index of instructional effectiveness.

Cranton, P. A., and Smith, R. A. "A New Look at the Effect of Course Characteristics on Student Ratings of Instruction." *American Educational Research Journal*, 1986, *23*, 117-128.

This study examined the effects of several course characteristics on student ratings of instructor effectiveness. When analyses were conducted at a departmental level, considerable variation in the relationships between such factors as class size and course level on student ratings was reported.

Crooks, T. J., and Kane, M. T. "The Generalizability of Student Ratings of Instructors: Item Specificity and Section Effects." *Research in Higher Education*, 1981, *15*, 305-313.

This study applied generalizability theory to determine the relative stability of student ratings over different course sections and different items. The study found that ratings were consistent across sections, but both number and type of rating items produced variability in the degree of generalizability. The authors recommend careful examination of the validity of items, but they overgeneralize their results when they suggest that one global rating item is sufficient for valid ratings.

Dowell, D. A., and Neal, J. A. "A Selective Review of the Validity of Student Ratings of Teaching." *Journal of Higher Education*, 1982, *53*, 51-62.

This review looks at six validity studies selected on the basis of methodology. It provides an excellent discussion of several difficulties in the evaluation of validity, and it concludes that many other studies are uninterpretable and that the validity of student ratings is modest and variable.

Doyle, K. O., Jr. *Evaluating Teaching*. Lexington, Mass.: Lexington Books, 1983.

This extensive resource on the topic is laudable for its attempts to incorporate historical perspective and some of the philosophical underpinnings of evaluation into a discussion of recent research. It provides a substantial discussion of methodological issues.

DuCette, J., and Kenney, J. "Do Grading Standards Affect Student Evaluation of Teaching? Some New Evidence on an Old Question." *Journal of Educational Psychology*, 1982, *74*, 308-314.

Contrary to other recent studies, this article concludes that student ratings are somewhat determined by the grade a student expects to receive. This effect may be emphasized in required core courses that are perceived negatively by students.

Eble, K. E., and McKeachie, W. J. *Improving Undergraduate Education Through Faculty Development: An Analysis of Effective Programs and Practices.* San Francisco: Jossey-Bass, 1985.

This book offers a close analysis of a wide variety of faculty development programs in many different colleges and universities. It furnishes a compendium of useful activities, as well as reactions of faculty, a look at the relationship of development to evaluation, and practical guidelines for effective programs.

Erdle, S., and Murray, H. G. "Interfaculty Differences in Classroom Teaching Behaviors and Their Relationship to Student Instructional Ratings." *Research in Higher Education,* 1986, *24,* 115–127.

This article finds differences in the frequency of certain teaching behaviors by faculty in different disciplines and a similar pattern of correlation between teaching behaviors and student ratings across all disciplines. Behaviors found to correlate with student ratings are reminiscent of commonly identified dimensions underlying effective instruction.

Erdle, S., Murray, H. G., and Rushton, J. P. "Personality, Classroom Behavior, and Student Ratings of College Teaching Effectiveness: A Path Analysis." *Journal of Educational Psychology,* 1985, *77,* 394–407.

Using path analysis, the authors provide evidence of relations among personality characteristics of the instructor, classroom behavior of the instructor, and student ratings of teaching effectiveness.

Feldman, K. A. "Seniority and Experience of College Teachers as Related to Evaluations They Receive from Students." *Research in Higher Education,* 1983, *18,* 3–124.

This is an in-depth review of the interrelationships among instructor rank, age, years of experience, and student evaluations. While the majority of studies show no relationship, those studies that do find relationships are consistent in pattern. Differences in findings may be due to underestimation, curvilinearity, the instructional dimension assessed, and which seniority variable is used. While relationship is weak overall, it should not be dismissed.

Feldman, K. A. "The Perceived Instructional Effectiveness of College Teachers as Related to Their Personality and Attitudinal Characteristics: A Review and Synthesis." *Research in Higher Education,* 1986, *24,* 139–213.

This article offers a detailed review of the relationship between instructor personality and rated effectiveness. Additionally, comparisons are made between student ratings of effectiveness and instructors' self-report on personality inventories. While relationships are found between perceived personality traits and rated effectiveness, a more tentative relation is found when these traits are assessed using the instructor's self-report.

Gibbs, G., Habeshaw, S., and Habeshaw, T. *Fifty-Three Interesting Things to Do in Your Lectures.* Bristol, England: Technical and Educational Services, 1984.

This informal guide provides simple suggestions for the improvement of teaching, ranging from methods for organizing the lecture and improving student note-taking to the informal assessment of student achievement.

Howard, G. S., Conway, C. G., and Maxwell, S. E. "Construct Validity of Measures of College Teaching Effectiveness." *Journal of Educational Psychology,* 1985, *77,* 187–196.

This interesting article applies multitrait-multimethod analysis and confirmatory factor analysis to the determination of the construct validity of alternative measures of teaching effectiveness. The authors underscore the need for multiple measures of a construct, and they point out problems in the criterion validation of teaching effectiveness.

Howard, G. S., and Maxwell, S. E. "Correlation Between Student Satisfaction and Grades: A Case of Mistaken Causation?" *Journal of Educational Psychology,* 1980, *72,* 810–820.

This article uses a path analytic approach to model the potential causal relations mediating student satisfaction in two studies. In both studies, the direct causal influence of grades on student satisfaction (the leniency-bias hypothesis) was found to be minimal.

Howard, G. S., and Maxwell, S. E. "Do Grades Contaminate Student Evaluations of Instruction?" *Research in Higher Education,* 1982, *16,* 175–188.

A study using cross-lagged panel correlation analysis provided no support for the hypothesis of a grading leniency bias in student ratings.

Levinson-Rose, J., and Menges, R. J. "Improving College Teaching: A Critical Review of Research." *Review of Educational Research,* 1981, *51,* 403–434.

This critical review looks at seventy-one research reports that used various interventions to improve instruction. Studies are categorized by type and then evaluated according to subjective criteria. Implications for the relationship between intervention and instructional improvement and for research and practice are made.

McKeachie, W. J. *Teaching Tips: A Guidebook for the Beginning College Teacher.* Lexington, Mass.: Heath, 1986.

This updated edition of the perennial classic on teaching improvement is an excellent resource for either the beginning or experienced college or university instructor. It provides discussion and suggestions on varied aspects of the instructional process from course design and organization to the assignment of grades and the evaluation of instructional effectiveness.

Marsh, H. W. "The Influence of Student, Course, and Instructor Characteristics in Evaluations of University Teaching." *American Educational Research Journal,* 1980, *17,* 219–237.

This article describes a prototypical study of relationships among student ratings of effectiveness and potentially confounding background characteristics (such as class size, expected grade, and so on). Sixteen characteristics were found to have only a negligible impact on student ratings.

Marsh, H. W. "Validity of Students' Evaluations of College Teaching: A Multitrait-Multimethod Analysis." *Journal of Educational Psychology,* 1982, *74,* 264–279.

Using instructor self-rating and student rating, this article finds stable dimensions underlying both sets of ratings. Multitrait-multimethod (MTMM) analysis provided evidence of both convergent and divergent validity. The use of empirically derived multifactor rating scales is recommended.

Marsh, H. W. "Students' Evaluations of University Teaching: Dimensionality, Reliability, Validity, Potential Biases, and Utility." *Journal of Educational Psychology,* 1984, *76,* 707–754.

Although not useful as a comprehensive review of the student evaluation literature, this article offers a good review of previous work by Marsh and colleagues, as well as a thought-provoking treatment of suggestions for a multifaceted conceptualization of teaching effectiveness and directions for future research in the area.

Marsh, H. W., and Hocevar, D. "The Factorial Invariance of Student Evaluations of College Teaching." *American Educational Research Journal,* 1984, *21,* 341–366.

This article provides additional support for the multidimensionality and validity of student ratings on a sample of instructors teaching the same course over a four-year period. MTMM analysis and confirmatory factor analysis were used to provide evidence of validity and generalizability of student ratings.

Millman, J. (ed.). *Handbook of Teacher Evaluation.* Beverly Hills: Sage, 1981.

This major resource on the evaluation of teaching was published in cooperation with the National Council on Measurement in Education.

It includes seventeen invited chapters on three major aspects of instructional evaluation: (1) context, criteria, and purposes of evaluation; (2) sources of evaluative information, including self, student, and peer evaluation, interviews, observation, student achievement, and indirect measures; and (3) systemic use of evaluative information, including instructional development, evaluation for administrative decision making, and the political and legal contexts of evaluation.

Murphy, K. R., Balzer, W. K., Kellam, K. L., and Armstrong, J. G. "Effects of the Purpose of Rating on Accuracy in Observing Teacher Behavior and Evaluating Teacher Performance." *Journal of Educational Psychology*, 1984, *76*, 45–54.

This study used videotaped lectures to examine the impact of the stated purpose of ratings on accuracy of rating. Results indicated that purpose did not have an effect on the overall level of rating or on rating accuracy.

O'Hanlon, J. O., and Mortensen, L. "Making Teacher Evaluation Work." *Journal of Higher Education*, 1980, *51*, 664–672.

Although brief and certainly less than exhaustive, this article offers a good list of suggestions for the improvement of the evaluation process.

Overall, J. U., and Marsh, H. W. "Students' Evaluation of Instruction: A Longitudinal Study of Their Stability." *Journal of Educational Psychology*, 1980, *72*, 321–325.

This article examines the stability of student ratings at least one year after course completion. The findings demonstrated that end-of-course ratings are quite similar to retrospective ratings provided by the same students.

Rotem, A., and Glasman, N. S. "On the Effectiveness of Student's Evaluative Feedback to University Instructors." *Review of Educational Research*, 1979, *49*, 497–511.

This is an important article for its early criticisms of the methodological shortcomings of studies of instructional improvement. While some conclusions are contradicted by more recent reviews, the suggestions for future research remain useful.

Seldin, P. *Changing Practices in Faculty Evaluation: A Critical Assessment and Recommendations for Improvement.* San Francisco: Jossey-Bass, 1984.

This book reviews the results of the author's nationwide surveys on evaluation practices and attitudes, discusses trends in evaluation practices, and makes suggestions for improvement of evaluation systems.

Stevens, J. J., and Aleamoni, L. M. "The Use of Evaluative Feedback for Instructional Improvement: A Longitudinal Perspective." *Instructional Science,* 1985, *13,* 285-304.

This quasi-experimental study emphasized the importance of tracking the course of instructional improvement over a protracted time period. The authors criticize the instructional improvement literature for extremely short durations of study.

Wilson, R. C. "Improving Faculty Teaching: Effective Use of Student Evaluations and Consultants." *Journal of Higher Education,* 1986, *57,* 196-211.

This article provides a detailed description of a consultation program designed to improve faculty effectiveness. It offers additional support for the finding that feedback of student ratings is not sufficient to produce meaningful instructor improvement but that additional consultation shows promise. It is quite useful for its description of the consultative process.

Joseph J. Stevens is research associate in the Office of Instructional Research and Development and adjunct professor of psychology at the University of Arizona.

Index

A

Abrami, P. C., 27, 28, 30, 83–84
Administrators, viewpoint of, 76–77
Aleamoni, L. M., 2, 3, 7, 25, 26, 27, 28, 29, 30, 31, 33, 34, 36, 38, 43, 46, 48, 49, 54, 58, 60, 64, 75, 78, 79, 81, 84, 91
Arizona, University of: conference at, 1; instruction weighted at, 76–77; student ratings at, 28
Armstrong, J. G., 90
Arreola, R. A., 1, 2, 39, 42n, 46, 65, 74
Assignments, ideas on giving, 18–21

B

Baldwin, R., 7, 31
Balzer, W. K., 90
Banz, M. L., 84
Basow, S. A., 84–85
Bavry, J. L., 23
Beatty, W. W., 28, 31
Berger, W. G., 28, 30–31
Bergquist, W. H., 58, 60, 64
Bess, J. L., 61–62, 64
Blackburn, R. T., 62, 64
Brandenburg, D. G., 7, 30
Braskamp, L. A., 5, 7, 85
Braunstein, D. N., 49, 54

C

Cadwell, J., 85
California at Berkeley, University of: Council on Educational Development at, 9, 17, 22; improving teaching at, 9–23; Teaching Evaluation Consultation Service (TECS) at, 9, 13, 21; Teaching Innovation and Evaluation Services (TIES) at, 9, 18
California at Los Angeles, University of, student ratings at, 28
Carnegie Commission, 81
Carnegie-Mellon University, colleague evaluations at, 49

Centra, J. A., 2, 33, 38, 47, 49, 53, 54, 55, 58, 62, 64, 85
Change, and feedback, 59–60
Cincinnati, University of, colleague evaluations at, 49–50
Clark, M. J., 62, 64
Cohen, P. A., 3, 7, 33, 34, 38, 49, 54, 85–86
Cohen, S. A., 28, 30–31
Colleagues, evaluation by, 25, 26–27, 49–50
Community colleges: analysis of faculty evaluation model for, 65–74; background on, 65–66; conclusion on, 74; faculty roles in, 66–68; implementation in, 68–72
Consultants: emeritus, 21; for improving teaching, 9–23; and student ratings, 34, 36; value of, 5, 6–7. See also Feedback
Conway, C. G., 88
Cooper, C. R., 26, 31
Costin, F., 26, 27, 31
Course/Instructor Evaluation Questionnaire, 28
Cranton, P. A., 86
Crooks, T. J., 86

D

Daugherty, M., 7, 31, 63, 64
Davis, B. G., 23
Deming, W. E., 25, 26, 28, 31
Dienst, E. R., 23
Distenfeld, M. S., 84–85
Dowell, D. A., 86
Doyle, K. O., Jr., 86
Drucker, A. J., 27–28, 31
DuCette, J., 86

E

Eble, K. E., 87
Edjerly, J., 51, 55
Educational Testing Service (ETS), 28, 51

Erdle, S., 87
Evaluation of instruction: analysis of, 3-7; approaches to, 75-78; appropriate techniques in, 4-6; background on, 3-4, 47-48, 65-66; class interviews for, 5; by colleagues, 25, 26-27, 49-50; composite ratings for, 70-73; comprehensive systems for, 77-78; conclusions on, 74, 79-81; consultants for, 5, 6-7, 9-23, 34, 36; defined, 40-41; and definitions of good teaching, 50-51; factions and, 54; as feedback process, 57-64; formative and summative, 47-55; for general factors, 5; guidelines for, 44-45; history and future of, 80-81; implementation of, 68-72; matrix for, 41-43, 68-69; in midsemester, 58; models of, 6-7, 65-74; with peer observations, 5; for personnel purposes, 4, 5, 6, 72-74; politics of, 53-54; purposes of 57; of research and scholarship, 52-53; role-by-source matrix for, 41-43; self-, 6; sources and information on, 83-91; specific information for, 4-5; student government role in, 39-46; with student ratings, 5, 48-49; student role in, 41-43; and teacher-designed examinations, 51-52; themes in, 79-80; uses of, 4

F

Faculty: cognitive state of, 34-36, 37; conveying ideas to, 13-17; examinations designed by, 51-52; ideas from, 9-13; role assessing for, 67-68; role determining and weighting for, 66-67; self-awareness by, 62-63; and student life cycles, 61-62; and student ratings, 25-31; viewpoint of, 75-76
Faculty evaluation. See Evaluation of instruction
Faculty Self-Description of Teaching, 13-16
Feedback: analysis of, 57-64; background on, 57; and change, 59-60; concept of, 58; evaluation versus, 58-59; individualized, 60-62; and instructional improvement, 59; recommendations on, 63; and self-awareness, 62-63
Feldman, K. A., 87
Florida, colleague evaluations in, 49
Fredericksen, N., 51, 52, 55
Frey, P. W., 28, 31

G

Gaff, J. G., 23, 61, 64
Gage, N. L., 58, 64
Gibb, J. R., 59, 64
Gibbs, G., 88
Gil, D. H., 2, 57, 64
Glasman, N. S., 33, 38, 90
Goldschmid, M. L., 57, 64
Grades, and student evaluations, 26, 29
Graham, M. H., 29, 30
Grasha, A. F., 49, 55
Greenough, W. T., 26, 31
Grush, J. E., 27, 31
Guthrie, E. R., 26, 31, 48, 55

H

Habeshaw, S., 88
Habeshaw, T., 88
Hexner, P. Z., 28, 30, 33, 38, 48, 54
Hocevar, D., 89
Howard, G. S., 88
Hsu, Y. M., 28, 31

I

Illinois, University of, student ratings at, 26, 27, 28, 29
Individual Teacher Profiles, 21-22
Instructional Development and Effectiveness Assessment, 28
Instructional improvement. See Teaching

J

Jenkins, J., 85

K

Kane, M. T., 86
Kansas State University, student-rating form at, 28

Kant, I., 51
Kellam, K. L., 90
Kenney, J., 86
Klein, G. A., 49, 54
Kohen, E., 7
Kulik, C.L.C., 5, 7, 33, 34, 38
Kulik, J. A., 5, 7, 33, 34, 38

L

Lancaster, O. E., 13
Leonard, D. W., 28, 31
Leventhal, L., 27, 30, 84
Levinson-Rose, J., 88
Lin Y.-G., 7, 31, 58, 63, 64
Linsky, A. S., 27, 31

M

McGuire, C. H., 51-52, 55
McKeachie, W. J., 1, 3, 6, 7, 28, 29, 31, 33, 34, 38, 48, 49, 55, 58, 63, 64, 87, 88-89
Marsh, H. W., 27, 28, 31, 33, 34, 38, 48, 55, 89, 90
Maxwell, S. E., 88
Mayberry, P. W., 7
Means, R. S., 28, 31
Menges, R. J., 26, 31, 88
Michigan, University of, instructional evaluation at, 6-7, 29
Miller, M. T., 49, 55
Millman, J., 33, 38, 48, 55, 89-90
Milton, O., 51, 55
Minute papers, for student understanding, 11-12
Mizener, D. A., 84
Moffett, M., 7, 31, 63, 64
Mortensen, L., 90
Murphy, K. R., 90
Murphy, V. A., 28, 30
Murray, H. G., 87

N

National Conference on Instructional Improvement and Evaluation Techniques for Colleges and Universities, 1
National Council on Measurement in Education, 89
National Governors' Association, 81

Neal, J. A., 86
Neigler, C., 7, 31
Nork, J., 7, 31

O

O'Hanlon, J. O., 90
O'Neal, E. C., 58, 64
Ory, J. C., 7, 85
Overall, J. U., 34, 38, 90

P

Pachla, M., 49, 54
Pambookian, H. S., 58, 64
Perry, R. P., 27, 30, 84
Personal Teaching Guide, 22-23
Personnel decisions, evaluation for, 4, 5, 6, 72-74
Petrosky, A., 26, 31
Phillips, S. R., 58, 60, 64
Piper, D., 53, 55
Powell, R. S., 58, 64
Purdue University, student ratings at, 27-28, 48

R

Remmers, H. H., 27-28, 31, 48, 55
Research and scholarship, evaluation of, 52-53
Rippey, R. M., 57, 64
Rodgers, J. L., 84
Rotem, A., 33, 38, 90
Rushton, J. P., 87

S

Schwenk, T., 59, 64
Selding, P., 90
Sheffield, E. F., 28, 31
Smith, R. A., 86
Southern Regional Education Board (SREB), 68
Spencer, R. E., 27, 31
Stallings, W. M., 27, 31
Stevens, J. J., 1, 29, 31, 33, 34, 36, 38, 83, 91
Straus, M. A., 27, 31
Student Description of Teaching, 9-11, 13, 22, 28
Student evaluation, defined, 40-41. See also Student ratings

Student government, evaluation role of, 39-46
Student Instructional Report, 28
Student ratings: analysis of, 25-31; background on, 33-34; concerns about, 25-26; conclusions on, 29-30, 37-38; and credibility, 43-44; defined, 40-41; effectiveness of, 26, 29, 33-34; evaluation with, 5, 48-49; and extraneous variables, 26, 28-29; history of, 39-40; for instructional improvement, 26, 29, 33-38, 49; instruments for, 28, 33; as popularity contest, 25, 27; purposes of, 33, 39-40; reliability and validity of, 26, 28, 33, 48-49; research on, 26-29
Students: class interviews of, 5; evaluation role of, 41-43; and faculty life cycles, 61-62; immaturity of, 25, 26; perspective of, 26, 27-28

T

Tauxe, C., 17n, 21, 23
Teaching: compendium of ideas for, 21-22; definitions of good, 50-51; elements of, 42; evaluation of, 3-7; evaluation of as feedback, 57-64; factors influencing improvement of, 34-36; feedback for improving, 59; improving 9-23; methods of, 50-51; modified ways to improve, 17-23; process in changing, 36-37; sample ideas for, 12-13; student ratings of, 25-31, 33-38, 49; system for improving, 36-37
Teaching Idea Packets (TIPs), 18-21, 22

U

Unions, and faculty evaluation, 66, 70
United Kingdom, politics of evaluation in, 53

W

Walz, M., 7, 31
Washington, University of, student ratings at, 28, 48
White, W. F., 28, 31
Whitman, N., 59, 64
Wilson, R. C., 1, 9, 11n, 16n, 17n, 21, 23, 28, 91
Wood, L., 23
Wotruba, T. R., 50, 55
Wright, P. L., 50, 55

Y

Yimer, M., 26, 28, 30